D0145856

jutland 1916

clash of the dreadnoughts

CHARLES LONDON

jutland 1916

clash of the dreadnoughts

Praeger Illustrated Military History Series

Westport, Connecticut
London

Library of Congress Cataloging-in-Publication Data

London, Charles.
    Jutland 1916: clash of the dreadnoughts / Charles London.
        p. cm – (Praeger illustrated military history, ISSN 1547-206X)
    Originally published: Oxford: Osprey, 2000.
    Includes bibliographical references and index.
    ISBN 0-275-98293-9 (alk. paper)
    1. Jutland, Battle of, 1916. I. Title. II. Series.
    D582.J8L66   2004
    940.4'56–dc22   2003066247

British Library Cataloguing in Publication Data is available.

First published in paperback in 2000 by Osprey Publishing Limited, Elms Court,
Chapel Way, Botley, Oxford OX2 9LP. All rights reserved.

Copyright © 2004 by Osprey Publishing Limited

Library of Congress Catalog Card Number: 2003066247
ISBN: 0-275-98293-9
ISSN: 1547-206X

Praeger Publishers, 88 Post Road West, Westport, CT 06881
An imprint of Greenwood Publishing Group, Inc.
www.praeger.com

Printed in China through World Print Ltd.

The paper used in this book complies with the Permanent Paper Standard issued
by the National Information Standards Organization (Z39.48-1984).

10 9 8 7 6 5 4 3 2 1

ILLUSTRATED BY: Howard Gerrard

CONTENTS

KEY TO MILITARY SYMBOLS

XXXXX	XXXX	XXX	XX	X
ARMY GROUP	ARMY	CORPS	DIVISION	BRIGADE
III	II	I		
REGIMENT	BATTALION	COMPANY	INFANTRY	CAVALRY
ARTILLERY	ARMOUR	MOTORIZED	AIRBORNE	SPECIAL FORCES

The ship that gave its name to a
generation of battleships:
HMS *Dreadnought*, seen in 1914
when she was flagship of the
4th Battle Squadron. Powered by
turbines, capable of higher
sustained speeds than
reciprocating machinery, and
armed with 12 x 12-in (305 mm)
guns, this revolutionary warship
rendered all contemporary
battleships obsolete. (IWM)

INTRODUCTION

'Be pleased to inform the Lords Commissioners of the Admiralty that the German High Sea Fleet was brought to action on 31 May 1916, to the westward of the Jutland Bank, off the coast of Denmark'

Admiral Sir John Jellicoe, Battle of Jutland Despatch

Vizeadmiral Reinhard Scheer ordered full speed. Thick jets of black smoke gushed from the funnels of 22 battleships. At the head of his line, four König class battleships surged forward, turbines exceeding the ships' previously recorded top speeds. Somewhere ahead, the battle cruisers of Vizeadmiral Hipper's *Aufklärungsgruppe* (reconnaissance division) were engaged in a running fight with British battle cruisers and a lone squadron of Dreadnoughts.

It was the opportunity for which Scheer and his fleet had trained all their professional lives. Since 1914 the fleet had waited, outnumbered by the British, but hoping to intercept an isolated squadron. Now opportunity beckoned. The Königs had already traded long-range shots with four British battleships. The British put about and steamed north at top speed. A single hit would leave them at the mercy of the *Hochseeflotte* (High Sea Fleet). The atmosphere on the bridge of Scheer's flagship, *Friedrich der Große,* was one of triumphant anticipation.

In the excitement, no one voiced any curiosity that the British were shaping a course north for Norway instead of directly away. Moments later, the horizon sparkled as each British battleship brought its guns to bear. The Royal Navy's Grand Fleet – the largest force of battleships in the world – was deployed in a concave arc dead ahead. Scheer had blundered into the greatest ambush in naval history.

What happened next remains highly contentious. Did Admiral Jellicoe, the British commander-in-chief, squander the chance of a lifetime? Did Scheer outmanoeuvre his terrible enemy, or just brazen out the subsequent 'battle of the historians'?

The British and Germans could not even agree on the name of the battle: to the Royal Navy it is 'Jutland', to Scheer and his men, 'the Skagerrak'. The only common ground has been Winston Churchill's celebrated line from *World Crisis*, that Jellicoe was 'the only man on either side who could lose the war in an afternoon'. Like many Churchillian aphorisms, the image is so powerful that it is repeated uncritically in book after book; but he was exaggerating for dramatic effect.

The only clash between the British and German battle fleets during the First World War was the biggest battleship action of all time. It was the last fleet engagement to be decided by surface action alone. There were no submarines present, and aircraft had no more than a minor peripheral influence.

ORIGINS OF
THE CAMPAIGN

I n 1888 Wilhelm II became King of Prussia and Emperor of Germany, an autocrat at the head of a nation in the throes of its industrial revolution. The German population grew by 60 percent in the 40 years after unification in 1871. Manufacturing output soared, cities expanded and, by 1914 the industrial working class had grown to 33 percent of the population. Pressure for social and political change gathered pace.

Within two years Wilhelm had dismissed the highly experienced Chancellor Otto von Bismarck, describing himself as 'Officer of the Watch of the Ship of State'. The nautical language was typical: Wilhelm spent an inordinate amount of time aboard his royal yacht, dressed in an admiral's uniform. His inspiration was Captain Alfred T. Mahan's celebrated *The Influence of Sea Power Upon History*, a disastrously influential analysis of the rise of the British Empire. Putting the cart before the horse, Mahan argued that colonies were the key to world power, providing both natural resources and markets for finished goods. To conquer and preserve them against other powers required a modern battle fleet. Mahan sought to create a modern blue water fleet in place of the United States Navy's motley assortment of coastal defence vessels: to challenge the naval monopoly the British had enjoyed since 1815.

Until Kaiser Wilhelm II inspired the creation of a 'blue-water navy' to challenge the British, the fleet had a very limited role in the military plans of the German empire. The *Hagen* was one of the six Siegfried class coastal defence ships built between 1888 and 1894 and modernised 1898–1904. Displacing 3,741 tons, they were armed with 3 x 9-in. (240 mm) guns. (IWM)

The first German battle cruiser set the pattern for the rest. The *Von der Tann* carried 11-in. (280 mm) guns compared to the 12-in. (305 mm) guns of the British Invincible class, but her main armour belt was 10-in. (254 mm) thick compared to 6-in. (150 mm). The first German capital ship to be powered by turbines, she could make 29 knots. (IWM)

Mahan's words ringing in his head, Kaiser Wilhelm demanded the construction of an ocean-going fleet, to provide worldwide diplomatic leverage in a way the German army could not. This was the end game of the colonial period, the great powers assigning themselves the last parts of Africa and Asia. The young German empire was determined to have its 'place in the sun': markets for its industry and 'living space' to absorb its population growth. It would not be the last time Germany prepared for war on the basis of a bogus political theory.

During the 1950s it was said that there was no international crisis so grave, no situation so serious, that a few, well-chosen words from United States Secretary of State John F. Dulles could not make worse. Kaiser Wilhelm shared this uncanny ability. He telegraphed his support for President Kruger on the eve of the Boer War. Cooler heads in Berlin questioned whether the friendship of the Transvaal was worth the enmity of the British Empire. His posturing stimulated France to conscript over 95 percent of draft-eligible men, creating an army almost the size of Germany's despite its smaller population. German intervention in a series of international crises prompted an Anglo-French entente and a Franco-Russian defence pact. His determination to construct a battle fleet that challenged the Royal Navy poisoned Anglo-German relations.

The naval arms race was masterminded by Admiral Alfred von Tirpitz. With his bristling twin forked beard, he looked a bluff sea dog, but was a far less straightforward creature. He sold the policy to the German establishment as a safety device to control the proletariat, to banish the spectre of socialism. By investing in a battle fleet, the cyclical economics of 'boom and bust' would be controlled: government orders to heavy industry meant guaranteed work, no more dangerous periods with laid-off workers inflating their political demands. For his master, he added an anti-parliamentarian flavour to the Navy Bills: the proposals not only authorised the creation of a massive fleet, but the replacement of capital ships after 20 years. In order to sustain this enormous force the

The Grand Fleet at sea. Admiral Jellicoe was painfully conscious (post-war critics said too conscious) that the Grand Fleet was the sole guarantor of Britain's safety. Churchill said he was the only man on either side who could lose the war in an afternoon, but it bears repeating that Jellicoe had no need to hazard his battleships in order to crush the German fleet. The British already had free access to the high seas. (IWM)

kaiser, or his successor, would not have to go cap in hand to the Reichstag.

There was one problem with Admiral von Tirpitz's plan. It was founded on 'risk theory': no one would hazard a fight with the new German navy. When von Tirpitz's programme was complete, Germany would have a fleet so formidable that even the world's premier naval power (Britain) would shrink from an engagement. Even if it won, it would be so weakened that lesser fleets (France and/or Russia) would have the advantage. But whereas the 1890s had witnessed some fraught moments in Anglo-French and Anglo-Russian relations, significantly, Wilhelmine foreign policy drove these rivals together. Admiral von Tirpitz assumed the British would maintain fleets in the Mediterranean and the Far East, while Germany had its entire fleet in the North Sea. But the British left the Mediterranean policed by the French and the Pacific safeguarded by their new ally, Japan, whose annihilation of the Russian navy stunned the world in 1905.

Not only did the British concentrate at home, they accelerated the pace of their own construction. It is so obvious that it tends to be skated over, but the British Isles then (as now) imported more than half their food by sea. And at the turn of the century the British economy depended on the import of raw materials and their export as finished goods by sea. The nation was dependent on freedom of navigation: were it to be curtailed by blockade, political capitulation would follow. Since the British started from a position of massive numerical advantage, Germany had to considerably increase its building to match the pace of British construction.

In 1906 the British launched HMS *Dreadnought*, a revolutionary battleship that set the pattern for all subsequent capital ships. *Dreadnought*'s armament consisted of ten 12-in. (305 mm) calibre guns, with a secondary armament of 12-pdrs. for anti-torpedo boat defence. Her contemporaries shipped a baroque assortment of intermediate calibre weapons in casemates, sponsons or turrets, with a pair of 10-, 11-, 12- or 13- in. (254, 279, 305 or 330 mm) guns fore and aft. *Dreadnought*'s broadside was more than twice as heavy as the then standard battleships and, driven by turbines, she was several knots faster and more capable of sustained high speed. The triple expansion steam engines employed in other battleships were prone to breakdowns after several hours' hard steaming. *Dreadnought* was hailed as a landmark in warship design by all naval authorities. A lone dissenting voice was David Lloyd George, who, in his characteristicly eloquent manner, called the battleship 'a piece of wanton and profligate ostentation'.[1]

Dreadnought rendered all other battleships obsolete: traumatic enough for the Royal Navy, which had more than anyone else, but a hideous surprise to the Germans whose gleaming new squadrons were redundant. From 1906, the index of naval power was measured in 'Dreadnoughts'. Germany had to start again from scratch. For Admiral Sir Jackie Fisher, the mercurial iconoclast who inspired the completion of *Dreadnought* in 13 months, it was the crowning glory. He had battled to remove from the active list an accumulation of ancient vessels 'too slow to run away and too weak to fight'. He sought to incorporate the flood of technical developments into the Navy, to shake off the complacency evident in the long afterglow of the Battle of Trafalgar. The serried ranks of grey battleships that steamed to Scapa Flow in 1914 formed 'the Fleet that Jack built'. And if he had had his way, there would have been no enemy to fight: he had suggested that his Dreadnoughts should descend on Kiel to 'Copenhagen' the German fleet. (The Royal

Dreadnought was followed by three similar battleships, the Bellerophon class, laid down 1906–07. These were followed by three St Vincent class battleships which featured a modified armour layout. *Vanguard*, seen here, the last unit of the St Vincent class, was destroyed when her magazines exploded while at anchor in Scapa Flow in 1917. (Vickers)

Navy attacked and defeated the then neutral Danish fleet in April 1801 in anticipation of its joining the French. The action was prolonged to a victorious conclusion by Nelson's 'blind eye' signal.)

Fisher's restless genius also inspired the creation of an entirely new class of ships: 'battle cruisers'. The concept was touted from the beginning of the century, when cruisers had grown larger than contemporary – 'pre-Dreadnought' – battleships, and hulls stretched to accommodate the power plant necessary for speeds over 20 knots. On the heaviest 'armoured cruisers' armament rivalled that of weaker battleships, with 9.2-in. (234-mm) guns as a main armament and more than a dozen 6-in. guns, too. Fisher's battle cruisers trumped them all. With turbines delivering a top speed of 25 knots and eight 12-in. (305 mm) guns, the Invincible class could exploit their speed advantage to stay out of range of their opponents' lighter guns. Theory was triumphantly turned into practice in December 1914 when *Invincible* and *Inflexible* sank the German armoured cruisers *Scharnhorst* and *Gneisenau* off the Falkland Islands.

'Speed is armour', said Fisher. Unfortunately, when it came to building their battle cruisers, the Germans carried over the same emphasis on protection that characterised their Dreadnoughts. German battle cruisers were slower than British ones and carried lighter armament: 11-in. (280 mm) guns, compared to the British 12-in. (305 mm) for the first generation, *Von der Tann, Seydlitz, Moltke* and *Goeben*; 12- in. (305 mm) compared to 13.5-in. (343 mm) for the second (and final) series, *Derfflinger, Lutzow* and *Hindenburg*. The British 12-in. (305 mm) gunned battle cruisers had main belts only half the thickness of a typical German Dreadnought.

Ajax was one of the four battleships laid down by the British in 1910. The King George V class ships were modified Orions with improved 13.5-in. (343 mm) Mk V guns. The Treasury blocked naval demands to increase the secondary armament to 6-in. (150 mm) calibre in line with German practice. (Author's Collection)

H.M.S. AJAX. Battleship, 23,600 tons.
Cost £1,965,000. Length, 555 feet; Beam, 89 feet; Draught, 27½ feet; Speed, 21½ knots. Armed with Ten 13.5; Sixteen 4 in.; Four Small Quick Firing Guns, and Three Torpedo Tubes.

By summer 1914 when a Royal Navy squadron visited Kiel, tension appeared to have eased. The British battle fleet was substantially stronger than Germany's and the pace of construction had slackened. A few senior officers on both sides strove to get along, but the undercurrent of suspicion could not be concealed, even by the laborious formality of the proceedings. The murder of Archduke Franz Ferdinand then triggered a crisis that political leaders had neither the skill, nor desire, to defuse. Within weeks all the major continental powers were at war.

The Anglo-German naval race had been accompanied by venomous rhetoric, creating a climate of hostility that helped the minority 'war party' in the British cabinet bounce their colleagues into declaring war. The pretext was the German invasion of Belgium: it was politically expedient to enter the conflict for humanitarian reasons and the defence of international law. The reality was fear of German hegemony in Europe, triggered in no small measure by the creation of the High Sea Fleet.

The Royal Navy was already assembled. In March 1914 the new First Lord of the Admiralty, Winston Churchill, had announced the replacement of the summer exercises with a test mobilisation of the 3rd Fleet – vessels manned by maintenance parties and in wartime crewed by reservists. It culminated in a Royal review of the fleet at Spithead, testimony that British naval pre-eminence had been upheld. To reinforce the point, as the visiting German delegation left his flagship, Rear-Admiral Beatty ordered the band to play *Rule Britannia*.

As the European crisis worsened, Admiral Prince Louis of Battenberg countermanded the order for the fleet to disperse and reservists to return to their homes. (It was his last service of a distinguished career: he was soon forced out of office as British xenophobia reached such ridiculous heights that even German Shepherd dogs had to be re-named.) As the orders of battle reveal, the Royal Navy enjoyed a comfortable margin of superiority. Since the launch of the *Dreadnought* Germany had constructed 13 Dreadnoughts and had seven building, plus four battle cruisers and three building. The British had completed 20 Dreadnoughts with another 12 building, plus nine battle cruisers with one more building.

THE OPPOSING FLEETS

The Grand Fleet put to sea to cover the deployment of the British Expeditionary Force to France, but there was no reaction from the High Sea Fleet. There were no liaison arrangements between the German army and navy. The British fears of an immediate assault on cross-Channel communications were not realised.

Based at Scapa Flow in the Orkneys, the Grand Fleet presided over the naval blockade of Germany. The British were the first to violate pre-war agreements regarding the rights of neutral shipping, tightening restrictions to prevent cargo of any sort going to Germany. Time was on their side. The new battle cruiser *Tiger* was completed in October and joined the 1st BCS in November. Two new Iron Duke class Dreadnoughts, *Benbow* and *Emperor of India*, joined the 4th BS on 10 December. The first of a new class of 'fast battleships', oil-fuelled and armed with 15-in. (381 mm) guns, *Queen Elizabeth* was fitting-out when the war started, and completed in January 1915. Four sisterships were due to join the fleet, two in 1915 and two in early 1916. The first of a follow-on class of 15-in. (381 mm) gunned battleships, *Revenge* was due in early 1916 with three sisterships later in the year and another due in 1917. The Royal Navy also took over three battleships under construction for other countries. (Contracts included a clause that the British government could invoke to secure a compulsory purchase, with compensation.)

After the defeat of the German East Asia squadron, the Royal Australian Navy's flagship, the battle cruiser *Australia* joined the 2nd BCS in summer 1915. The three battle cruisers returned from the Mediterranean: Indomitable joined the Grand Fleet in December 1914; *Indefatigable* in February 1915; *Inflexible* in May 1915.

The *Revenge* was commissioned in February 1916 and became Admiral Burney's temporary flagship after the *Marlborough* was torpedoed at Jutland. On the morning after the battle she engaged a German zeppelin with her 15-in. (381 mm) main armament.

Three König class Dreadnoughts joined the High Sea Fleet in autumn 1914. Whereas the British had a dozen more battleships in varying states of completion, Germany had only laid down four more battleships and three battle cruisers. The battle cruiser *Derfflinger* was commissioned in 1914. *Lützow* was scheduled to join the fleet in October 1915 but was delayed by trouble with her turbines until 1916. *Bayern* was not commissioned until July 1916, *Baden* in February 1917; the others were never completed.

The High Sea Fleet was in the best shape at the end of 1914. Four British battle cruisers had been detached: *Inflexible* and *Invincible* were in the south Atlantic, where they avenged the defeat of a British squadron by the German East Asiatic Squadron; *Princess Royal* covered a Canadian troop convoy, *Indefatigable* was in the Mediterranean. One battleship had been lost; *Audacious* succumbed to a mine off Lough Swilly, laid by the German liner *Berlin*, operating as an auxiliary cruiser. Several British battleships were laid up with condenser defects every week, the consequence of hard steaming and the haste with which the newest ships had been commissioned. *Monarch* and *Conqueror* collided on 27 December and were sent to Devonport for repair.

The Grand Fleet

Officers and men alike (not to mention the general public) had an unshakeable conviction in the navy's moral and material superiority,

H.M.S. AGINCOURT.

British shipyards building to foreign accounts provided a windfall in 1914: under the terms of their contracts, two Turkish battleships and one Chilean were subject to compulsory purchase on the outbreak of war. Originally ordered by Brazil, but bought by Turkey as she neared completion, the *Sultan Osman-i Evvel* was incorporated in the Royal Navy as the *Agincourt*. Uniquely, she carried seven turrets on the centreline for a broadside of 14 x 12-in. (305 mm) guns. At Jutland she fired full salvoes, the spectacle looking 'like a Brock's benefit' according to one observer. (IWM)

reinforced by a hundred years of intervention ashore. British seamen signed on for 12 years. Some features of their lives would have been familiar to the men of Trafalgar: aboard the battle cruiser *Tiger*, ancient lumps of salted meat were towed behind the ship for 24 hours to soften them. Casemates were warmed by solid shot, heated in the furnace and placed in a bucket of sand. Captains no longer had the powers they enjoyed in Nelson's day, but some wielded authority in the same manner as the tyrants of nautical fiction. Most notorious was the fitness fanatic and pugilist Rear-Admiral Sir Robert Arbuthnot, Bart., who forced defaulters into the boxing ring where respect for their betters could be beaten into them. (He was ambushed ashore one dark night by three ratings, but hospitalised all of them.)

There were no major naval battles between Lissa (1866) and the Russo-Japanese war (1904–05). Few conclusions could be drawn from minor actions in the interlude. The poverty of evidence ensured that the feasibility of ramming was under discussion for 50 years. Warships evolved from wooden walls with primitive steam machinery, to steel vessels four times as fast, five times the size and carrying infinitely more firepower. Until 1904–05 there was little data to suggest what might happen in a fleet action. For most senior officers at Jutland, tactics were conditioned by their experiences of peacetime exercises. While a number of vocal officers demanded more warlike 'wargames', others were content to earn their promotion through smart ship handling and sparkling paintwork.

Fighting services seldom find themselves at peak efficiency after prolonged peace. Neither of the main battle fleets at Jutland had ever fired a shot in anger before. No senior commander had commanded a squadron of Dreadnoughts in battle. The Royal Navy had developed routines that could only have flourished in peacetime. Signalling had become the province of specialist officers. Successive revisions of the signal book produced a tome the size of a modern software manual and no more comprehensible. Captains grew accustomed to receive minutely detailed instructions. The movement of every ship, every squadron, was

The pace of technological change in the second half of the 19th century captured in one photograph. In the 1860s the Royal Navy's main strength consisted of 55 steam- and sail-powered ships of the line, externally little different from Nelson's time. In 1902 Vickers supplied the Royal Navy with its first Holland-type submarines. By the beginning of the 20th century, warships that took three years to build could be obsolete within a decade. (IWM)

choreographed from the flagship by a stream of flags and wireless telegraphy was in its infancy. The prevailing assumptions were that 'Admiral knows best' and 'Admiral knows all': four rings on the sleeve were the mark of omniscience.

The range of battleship main armament trebled between the 1880s and 1905. Speeds nearly doubled. Coal-burning ships produced their own smokescreen. In these circumstances, any system of signal flags was handicapped, but the British had burdened themselves with a particularly cumbersome one. A minority of officers addressed this issue, but they were ignored. The Grand Fleet went to war with a centralised command structure allied to a flawed communications system.

The Dreadnought battle squadrons of the Grand Fleet were based on Scapa Flow. This remote anchorage was the only one big enough to accommodate the whole fleet. However, it proved too far north for the fleet to prevent 'tip-and-run' raids by German cruisers on the east coast of England. The battle cruiser squadrons were transferred to Rosyth, from where they could intervene in good time, but this proved divisive. The battle cruiser fleet became a self-conscious élite. Its morale soared

British battle cruiser officers based at Rosyth could have a run ashore in Edinburgh, but recreational facilities at the main fleet base at Scapa Flow were few and far between. Allotments were maintained by some officers and petty officers at Scapa, providing a source of activity and a welcome supplement to uninspiring rations. (IWM)

to over-confidence after its two clashes with the Germans. A certain smugness crept into its relations with the rest of the fleet. There was nowhere to practise gunnery at Rosyth, however, and when battle cruisers visited Scapa for exercises their shooting was not up to standard.

Rear-Admiral Hood's 3rd BCS was ordered to Scapa for gunnery exercises in May 1916. To cover its absence, the battle cruiser fleet was reinforced with the four Queen Elizabeth class 'fast battleships' of the 5th BS (the fifth, *Queen Elizabeth*, was refitting). Thus, when the battle of Jutland occurred, the battle cruiser force was more powerful, but less co-ordinated. The replacement squadron was unfamiliar with the tactical ideas of the BCF and in the week they had together before the battle, the squadron commander, Rear-Admiral Evan-Thomas, never spoke to Beatty. Nor was there much visiting between the squadrons' captains.

British tactics at Jutland were laid down in *Grand Fleet Battle Orders*, a 70-page testimony to the centralisation of the Royal Navy. Issued by Admiral Jellicoe it was a combination of sailing orders and manoeuvres that expressed his emphasis on the big gun. He regarded the battleships as a single tactical entity: steaming in line of battle, with his flagship in the middle, pounding the enemy battle line. He resisted any notion that the Dreadnoughts might operate in several units, resenting Vice-Admiral Sir Doveton Sturdee for even venturing the suggestion. The fact that the line of battle stretched for over 7 miles (11 km) in its closest sailing order – not far off typical North Sea visibility – is not obvious from the neat diagrams that illustrate the *Grand Fleet Battle Orders*.

The ideal was the manoeuvre known as 'crossing the T': placing the battle line sideways to the enemy's line of advance, like the horizontal stroke of the letter 'T' capping the vertical one. Battleships in such a position could bring their full broadsides to bear against an enemy who could only fire back with the forward armament of his leading ships.

Both fleets regarded battleship gunnery as the decisive weapon, but there were new weapons to be taken into account. The torpedo represented a potent threat because it attacked ships below the waterline where damage was most dangerous, and protective measures were speculative; ranges and explosive power had increased faster than

The British pioneered the use of aircraft at sea, converting a number of merchant vessels into sea-plane carriers. The *Campania* was part of the Grand Fleet and carried a captive balloon in addition to aircraft. Her battle station was a mile off the disengaged side of the flagship, but her aerial observation was missed at Jutland because she never received the order to sail. She put to sea to follow the fleet, but Jellicoe ordered her back to port rather than send her alone through the waiting U-boat line. (IWM)

underwater protection could be tested. 'Destroyers' are so called because the British built 'Torpedo Boat Destroyers' in response to French 'Torpedo Boats' at the turn of the century. The former carried torpedoes too, but these were intended to drive off the smaller torpedo boats with their heavier gun armament. By 1914 differences between the types had blurred, but in general the British flotillas carried more guns and fewer torpedoes than their German equivalents. Destroyers had limited endurance, but their importance was such that neither battle fleet was prepared to risk sailing without them. At the battle of Tsushima, Japanese torpedo craft had sunk a number of Russian heavy ships during the night. The spectre of a massed torpedo attack was feared by battleship admirals as much as it was anticipated by destroyer captains.

Submarines, making a terrifying debut in 1914, were an even greater mystery. On 22 September *U 9* sank the armoured cruisers *Aboukir*, *Hogue* and *Cressy* off the Dutch coast; 1,459 officers and men were lost. Dissident voices had predicted disaster if these old cruisers maintained the British presence in the Broad Fourteens, but surviving memos cite the threat from German surface forces. That the danger could come from beneath the waves occurred to no one, not even the captain of the *Cressy* who had commanded a submarine flotilla for three years.

Both sides planned to draw the enemy battle squadrons over a concentration of submarines as a preliminary to a fleet action. Both fleets shared a jitteriness, reacting to non-existent submarines. No submarines were present at Dogger Bank or Jutland, but many a lookout misinterpreted the breaking of a wave or a piece of flotsam for a periscope.

The Grand Fleet pioneered the use of aircraft at sea. The seaplane carrier *Engadine* was with the battle cruisers. The battle squadrons were accompanied by the converted liner *Campania* which had a double role. Seaplanes were set on the water by crane and hoisted in at the end of their flight. She was fitted with a kite balloon in November 1915: steaming a mile on the disengaged side of the flagship, she was intended to provide Jellicoe with a 'bird's-eye' view of the action. However, *Campania* missed the signal to leave harbour on 31 May.

The Grand Fleet enjoyed one priceless advantage at Jutland: British listening stations ashore could decipher German radio messages. The Germans used three code systems in 1914. The HVB (*Handeslverkehrsbuch*) was used for communication with merchant ships. The Royal Navy obtained a copy from a German merchantman caught in Melbourne at the outbreak of war, an Australian naval officer beating the German skipper to the secret compartment where the codes resided. On 26 August 1914 the cruiser *Magdeburg* ran aground off the Estonian coast. Russian cruisers arrived as her crew transferred to a destroyer, scuttling charges went off prematurely and three copies of the German warship signal code were captured. In a magnificent gesture of co-operation, copy 151 of the SKM (*Signalbuch der Kaiserlichen Marine*) was sent to Britain. The arrival of two Russian officers at Scapa in October and the nature of their mission was an open secret within the Grand Fleet, but no word of it reached Germany. Finally, on 30 November, a fishing trawler brought up a lead-lined chest off the Texel – the secret papers from the torpedo boat *S 119*, jettisoned as she went under during a destroyer action on 17 October. The haul included the third German naval code, the VB (*Verkehrsbuch*), issued to the light forces.

On 31 May 1916 Admiral Scheer planned to entice the British into battle by appearing off the Norwegian coast. Thanks to the team in Room 40 of the Admiralty's Old Building, the Grand Fleet left harbour four hours before the High Sea Fleet. If the system worked smoothly, Admiral Jellicoe would be passed copies of his opponent's signals within an hour or so of transmission.

At 1716hrs on 30 May 1916 Admirals Jellicoe and Beatty received a signal informing them that the High Sea Fleet would put to sea the following morning. Jellicoe was ordered to concentrate the Grand Fleet off the Long Forties, some 100 miles (161 km) east of Aberdeen. A Royal Marine aboard *Tiger* noted in his diary, 'Just another sweep, I expect'.

By 2300hrs the battle cruisers and the 5th Battle Squadron had departed Rosyth and the Grand Fleet was steaming down from the Orkneys. In total, 28 battleships, nine battle cruisers, eight armoured cruisers, 26 light cruisers, 78 destroyers, one seaplane carrier and a minelayer: 151 warships and over 60,000 men.

The *Hochseeflotte*

'It takes three years to build a ship, but three hundred to build a tradition', said Admiral Cunningham as he committed his depleted squadrons to the rescue of British forces from Crete in 1941. The High Sea Fleet had only seven years: not until 1907 was the Imperial Navy so styled. Its first commander-in-chief was the kaiser's brother, Admiral Prince Heinrich of Prussia. On the eve of the Dreadnought revolution it consisted of two squadrons, each of eight battleships, plus a reconnaissance squadron of three armoured and six light cruisers. A reserve fleet of eight old coastal defence ships, two elderly battleships and five cruisers supported it. Four battleships of the Kaiser class (completed 1898–1901) were reconstructing.

Only two fleets were larger: the United States Navy had 18 battleships completed after 1895; the British Royal Navy had 39, with a dozen older battleships in reserve. However, the German battle fleet was weaker than the numbers suggest. The Kaisers and the five units of the Wittlesbach class were armed with 9.4-in. (240 mm) guns (shell weight 309 lbs; 140 kg) but their potential opponents shipped 12-in. (305 mm) weapons (shell weight 850 lbs; 386 kg). The idea was to overwhelm the enemy with a hail of rapid fire – they carried 18 x 5.9-in. (150 mm) guns too – but the 'big gun revolution' rendered these ships obsolete.

The light cruiser *Magdeburg* ran aground off Estonia on 26 August 1914. Her commander and 57 crewmen were captured by the Russians, together with three copies of the main German signal code. One was sent to Britain, enabling the Royal Navy to decipher German radio traffic, a priceless advantage that would be sadly squandered. (IWM)

From 1907–14 the High Sea Fleet expanded so fast that the building yards could not keep pace. Nor could the tax system, which relied on alcohol and tobacco duties since the aristocracy opposed income tax reforms. Krupp's workforce grew from 50,000 to 100,000 from 1904–09. Heavy industry began to depend on government orders. In 1898 naval expenditure was less than a fifth of that lavished on the army; by 1913 it was just over half. At tremendous economic and political cost, Germany constructed ships faster than any nation except Britain.

In certain respects, the High Sea Fleet made up for its numerical inferiority by a qualitative advantage. German range finders proved quicker at establishing the range of a target. British naval budgets had funded the warships, but not the facilities to go with them, so battleships had to be designed for existing docks. The Germans approached the problem from the other end, creating the docks for the warships. With wider beams, their battleships were steadier gun platforms. They devoted a greater proportion of their displacement to protection than their British equivalents. This more than compensated for their lighter shells because British armour-piercing ammunition proved liable to break up on impact, rather than penetrate enemy armour. But the first German Dreadnoughts had triple expansion engines, not turbines, so required an extensive overhaul after a day or two's hard steaming; and they were slower, permitting the faster British to close or extend the range.

German sailors were mostly conscripts, recruited for three years. Every summer a new intake arrived, with no prior experience of the sea, to replace the class of men reaching the end of their term.

German officers were divided into the executive and engineering branches, the gap between them unbridgeable. In the High Sea Fleet nearly twice as many engineer officers had university degrees as sea officers, but social class was more important. A Dreadnought might have six engineer officers in charge of 400 men in the boiler and engine rooms. Not allowed in the *kasino* and excluded from social functions, they retaliated in 1917 by boycotting the kaiser's birthday festivities. In the Royal Navy engineers were combined with the military branch in 1915, although it took many years for the social gulf to narrow. In the High Sea Fleet the same innovation was discussed but ditched in 1917. They heaped petty indignities on the engineers and *Deck-Offiziere* (literally, 'deck officers', a junior class of officer unique to the German navy). To suggest that the High Sea Fleet was riven by class warfare in 1914 would be an exaggeration; its morale was high. Yet the fissures along which it disintegrated after Jutland were visible at the beginning.

The tactics and training of the High Sea Fleet were very similar to that of the Royal Navy. The big gun was the weapon of decision, torpedo boats and submarines were ancillaries. Engagement ranges beyond 6.2 miles (10 km) were regarded as impossible. The line of battle was treated as a single tactical entity, although with one key difference. The High Sea Fleet practised a manoeuvre whereby the line reversed course, each ship putting over her helm once the ship astern had begun to turn. The *Gefechtskehrtwendung* (battle about-turn) would be its salvation at Jutland, but its existence exposes a critical difference between the 'mindset' of the fleets. In its exhaustive repertoire of signals and manoeuvres, the Royal Navy had no such mechanism for breaking off an action.

THE WAR IN THE NORTH SEA 1914–15

On 28 August 1914 the British raided the Heligoland Bight where their submarines had observed the Germans' routine. Several cruisers were usually present, covering torpedo boats on anti-submarine patrol, but they were cut off from support at predictable intervals. When the British struck, the tide was too low over the bar at the entrance to the Jade Basin for German capital ships to cross. Although the British operation was amateurish – their own submarines were not told that British battle cruisers would be in the area – they emerged victorious. Beatty intervened in dramatic style: *Queen Mary* and *Lion* risked mines and U-boats to plunge into the wild mêlée in the mist. Three German cruisers were sunk, with heavy loss of life, including Konteradmiral Leberecht Maaß and his staff aboard the *Cöln*. The British stopped to take off the crew of the *Mainz*, which sank after a heroic fight, the prisoners including Oberleutnant zur see Wolfgang von Tirpitz. Winston Churchill had a message sent to his father, assuring him that his son was safe.

On 10 September, as transports continued to shuttle the BEF to France, the Grand Fleet steamed provocatively close to Heligoland, but the Germans remained in harbour. Admiral von Ingenohl had been ordered not to hazard his fleet, but after the Heligoland battle his officers prodded him into action. On 3 November he despatched a cruiser force to shell Yarmouth and lay mines off the port. Notwithstanding the loss of the armoured cruiser *Yorck*, which foundered in the Jade after striking stray mines on her return, von Ingenohl

Princess Royal, the Lion class battle cruiser second in Beatty's line at Jutland. The 'splendid cats' continued the trend for British battle cruisers to carry heavier guns than their German equivalents: they were armed with 8 x 13.5-in. (343 mm) guns. (IWM)

The British had won the naval race by 1914. During 1912–13 they laid down five units of the Queen Elizabeth class, of which only the nameship, seen here, missed Jutland. Their combination of enormous firepower (15 in./ 381 mm guns), excellent armour protection and high speed (24 knots) was unmatched by any German battleship and they would serve with distinction in both world wars. (IWM)

ordered a more ambitious raid for 16 November, later postponed to 16 December. Konteradmiral Hipper, flying his flag on *Seydlitz* led the battle cruisers *Moltke*, *Derfflinger*, and *Von der Tann*; the armoured cruiser *Blücher*; four light cruisers; and two torpedo boat flotillas to attack the English coast. The undefended towns of Scarborough and Whitby were bombarded. At Hartlepool a 6-in. (150 mm) shore battery hit *Blücher* and Hipper's flagship. But over 100 civilians were killed and the British press lambasted the Admiralty for failing to catch the 'baby-killers'.

Had the papers learned what really went on that night, heads would have rolled. Forewarned by Room 40, the Admiralty had set a trap. Vice-Admiral Beatty's battle cruisers, supported by the 2nd Battle Squadron, were placed to intercept the raiders. Beatty's cruiser screen clashed with Hipper's, but broke off action when a signal made to one of them was accidentally addressed to the whole squadron by Beatty's flag lieutenant. Who was more culpable – Lieutenant-Commander Seymour (for sending the signal) or Commodore Goodenough (for obeying it) – was hotly debated. Signalling errors were to be a standard feature of Beatty's engagements.

It was not only the British who squandered an opportunity. Unaware the Germans were out in force, the Admiralty sent a single squadron of British Dreadnoughts to support Beatty – and straight into the path of the High Sea Fleet. Destroyers screening Vice-Admiral Warrender's 2nd Battle Squadron met their German opposite numbers at 0515hrs, but Von Ingenohl convinced himself he faced a mass torpedo attack preparatory to a fleet engagement. He ordered his fleet to turn for home, abandoning Hipper without telling him. Ingenohl had brought the High Sea Fleet to within 10 miles (16 km) of a single British battle squadron, 14 German versus six British battleships: the 'dream scenario' that might have given Germany parity in capital ships. Admiral von Tirpitz wrote, 'Von Ingenohl had the fate of Germany in the palm of his hand. I boil with inward emotion whenever I think of it.' There were dark suggestions that von Ingenohl's English wife might account for his hesitancy and caution.

British officers were equally aghast at missing their chance. Beatty called it 'the blackest day of my life'. The British *Official History* is not noted for trenchant criticism, which makes Sir Julian Corbett's conclusion all the more damning: 'Two of the most efficient and

23

The Grand Fleet at sea. The line of battle could stretch for up to 10 miles (16 km), often more than the limit of visibility in the North Sea, but communications remained reliant on signal flags. Lopsided technical progress gave the Royal Navy a magnificent battle fleet but a cumbersome command system. (IWM)

powerful British squadrons, with an adequate force of scouting vessels, knowing approximately what to expect, and operating in an area strictly limited by the possibilities of the situation, had failed to bring to action an enemy who was operating in close conformity with our appreciation and with whose advanced screen contact had been established.'[2]

Von Ingenohl's chief-of-staff, Vizeadmiral von Eckermann, believed the reason the British seemed to be so well informed about German naval movements was that they were using 'spy trawlers' – radio-equipped and flying neutral flags. Hipper agreed. The Germans launched an operation to catch some of these mythical intelligence gatherers off the Dogger Bank.

On the afternoon of 23 January Hipper put to sea with *Seydlitz, Moltke, Derfflinger* and *Blücher* (*Von der Tann* was undergoing repairs), light cruisers *Graudenz, Rostock, Kolberg* and *Straslund*, and 18 torpedo boats. Their departure was known to the Admiralty which ordered Beatty's battle cruisers after them, with the Grand Fleet in support. Beatty and Hipper's light cruisers met shortly after dawn on Sunday 24 January. Hipper signalled the news that he was in contact with 'eight large ships' and von Ingenohl, still in port, ordered the battle fleet to raise steam and assemble in the Schillig Roads.

There were actually five British battle cruisers: *Lion, Tiger, Princess Royal, New Zealand* and *Indomitable*. The odds against him, Hipper turned for home. A stern chase ensued, but *Blücher*, at the rear of the German line, had neither the firepower nor the protection to shoot it out with battle cruisers. The British battle cruisers were also faster. *Lion* made a magnificent sight, pelting south at 27 knots, forward turrets firing at the unheard-of range of 10 nautical miles (20 km). Beatty ordered his ships to engage their opposite numbers, but *Tiger* joined *Lion* and fired on *Seydlitz*, leaving *Moltke* to make undisturbed practice.

This was like no pre-war exercise: the great ships were at full speed, firing as rapidly as they could. Near misses threw up towering columns of water. In *Lion*'s conning tower the spray led the navigating officer to don an oilskin. Prince George of Battenberg, commanding *New Zealand*'s fore turret, remembered, 'My range finder was useless; I was soaked through to the skin by the spray coming in through the slit in my hood, hitting

The second German battle cruiser, *Moltke*, was an improvement over *Von der Tann*. She shipped 10 x 11-in. (280 mm) guns with a higher muzzle velocity and carried her secondary armament higher for better performance in a seaway. She survived five heavy calibre hits at Jutland, escaping past the British during the night on her own. (IWM).

me in the face and then trickling down outside and inside my clothes, and I was frozen by the wind which came in with the spray.[3]

Blücher signalled that her engines were hit and fell astern. A shell penetrated her deck and exploded in the ammunition gangways that fed her port wing turrets. Propellant charges ignited in a chain reaction, the crews of both turrets burned to death. A similar disaster struck the *Seydlitz* when a 13.5-in. (343 mm) shell from *Lion* penetrated the rear barbette and exploded inside. Charges in the working chamber ignited, the flash roared into the gun house and ignited others there, immolating the crew. Fire spread down the hoists. The fumes drove men in the handing room to open the bulkhead door that gave access to 'C' turret's handing room. Charges ignited there and the connecting door to 'D' turret was blown open. Flames shot up into the gunhouse and down to the magazine. Sixty-two charges (13,200 lb; 6,000 kg of propellant) were ablaze before the magazines were flooded; 159 men were burned to death.

Lion and *Tiger* were hit repeatedly, *Lion* reduced to 15 knots after a shell stopped her port engine. Beatty was no longer able to control the action. Then he thought he saw a torpedo track and ordered his squadrons to turn away. Nevertheless, with four serviceable battle cruisers against the three German, the British should have been able to overwhelm them. But Beatty's flag signals were misinterpreted, his second-in-command Rear-Admiral Moore in *New Zealand* read two different hoists together and assumed Beatty's intention was to concentrate on the *Blücher* and give the others the chance to escape – which they did. Hipper was conscious that if any of his ships suffered engine damage they would be left helpless in the path of superior forces; his flagship had suffered severe damage and had expended three-quarters of her ammunition. *Blücher* fought to the last, capsizing at 1310hrs, three hours and twenty minutes after *Lion* opened fire. Tragically, the Zeppelin *L 5* bombed the British destroyers engaged in rescue operations. Her complement, increased by a draft from *Von der Tann*, was just over 1,000 men on board, but only 237 were saved.

British newspapers presented it as a great victory: the famous photograph of *Blücher* capsizing was on the front page of the Daily Mail. Two hundred German prisoners arrived in Edinburgh. Beatty was hailed as a new Nelson. In private, he seethed that another opportunity to wipe out the German battle cruisers had been let slip. Admiral Fisher wanted scalps, and thundered that 'any fool can obey orders'. He started by demanding Moore's court martial and ended by wanting him shot. The Admiralty settled on a sideways posting: on 8 February Moore was appointed to command a cruiser squadron in the Canaries (and did eventually gain promotion to full admiral). Beatty intervened to save Captain Pelly of the *Tiger*, whose shooting had been abysmal, but her gunnery officer, Lieutenant-Commander Bruce-Gardyne, was sacked. Unbidden, the ship's company manned the sides and cheered him as he left; his disgrace was not permanent as he ended the war in command of the *Lion*.

Recriminations in Germany were worse. A cabal of senior officers, led by Captain von Levetsow of the *Moltke* and von Egidy of the *Seydlitz* agitated for the removal of von Ingenohl. They had influence at court, with the army high command and with Chancellor von Bethmann Hollweg. Von Ingenohl had enemies in low places too: at Kiel and Wilhelmshaven housewives and children jeered him in the street. The head of the German *Admiralstab*, Admiral Hugo von Pohl, obtained von Ingenohl's removal, then surprised the plotters by engineering his own appointment to command the Fleet. Von Pohl had suggested that a submarine campaign against British merchant shipping, unfettered by the restrictions of international law, offered Germany its only realistic opportunity of success. Faithful to his Kaiser's determination to retain an intact fleet as a bargaining chip in eventual negotiations, he made just five sorties in the next ten months, none further than 120 miles (192 km) from Germany. Towards the end of 1915, he became ill; liver cancer was diagnosed in January 1916 and on the 24th he was replaced by Vizeadmiral Reinhard Scheer.

Von Tirpitz resigned from office in March, his alternate championing of a fleet action or a U-boat offensive having alienated every major political and military figure. 'He is leaving the sinking ship', commented the Kaiser.

THE OPPOSING COMMANDERS

Admiral Sir John Jellicoe fought Jutland still carrying the Chinese bullet he received when leading a bayonet charge in China. He planned to attack the High Sea Fleet with submarines and draw it over a minefield prior to destroying it in a gunnery action. Seaplane attacks on its bases were intended to tempt the Germans out for battle. His assumption that Admiral Scheer planned to attempt a similar ambush was entirely correct and governed his handling of the fleet at Jutland. (IWM)

Admiral John Rushworth Jellicoe

In 1913 Vice-Admiral Jellicoe, Second Lord of the Admiralty, commanded 'Red Fleet' – the aggressor forces, tasked with 'invading' England – in the Royal Navy's summer exercises. He outmanoeuvred the defending 'Blue Fleet' led by the Admiral of the Home Fleet, Sir George Callaghan. Indeed, the exercise was brought to a premature close. Jellicoe's troopships were in the Humber, the exercise staff judged his invasion a complete success and did not want to publicise the ease with which he had managed it.

In July 1914 60-year-old Admiral Callaghan was approaching retirement. The Admiralty, especially First Lord Winston Churchill, wished to have Jellicoe at the helm from the outset. Jellicoe was ordered to Scapa, bearing a letter to be opened in the presence of both men: his order to take command. To demur at replacing Callaghan, a personal friend, was understandable, but Jellicoe went beyond a conventional show of reluctance. He wired Churchill twice on arrival, arguing against his promotion, and twice more on 2 August, either side of a terse signal ('I can give you 48 hours you must be ready then') from the First Lord. Still he objected to taking over 'before I have a thorough grasp of Fleet and situation', wiring twice more the next morning before Churchill put an end to the exchange by signalling Callaghan, ordering him to hand over his command.

Jellicoe had refused the crown more times than Caesar. Yet his objection was to taking over at short notice. Aged 54 when he raised his flag at Scapa, he had been in the navy for 42 years. After two years at HMS *Britannia*, he went to sea in 1874 aboard the 17-gun frigate HMS *Newcastle*. A gunnery lieutenant in the *Monarch* in 1885, he won the Board of Trade Life Saving Medal for braving heavy seas in a small boat to rescue the crew of a sailing ship. In 1886 he dived in to save a seaman swept overboard from the *Colossus* during a gale at Spithead. An aggressive rugby player despite his slender stature, Jellicoe was not expected to survive the bullet he took while leading a bayonet charge during the Boxer rebellion. He recorded in his diary: 'After a bit Dr Sibbald came up and bandaged the wound and told me that he thought I was finished. I made my will on a bit of paper and gave it to my coxswain. I was spitting up a lot of blood and thought the wound probably mortal, so asked Pickthorn [another naval surgeon]...to rebandage me, if this was so. He said it was very dangerous and injected morphia.'

Jellicoe was fortunate to have survived until then: he was aboard Admiral Tryon's flagship when she was rammed and sunk by HMS *Camperdown* in 1893. Confined to his berth for a week with Malta Fever, Jellicoe staggered on deck just before *Victoria* capsized.

He was promoted captain on 1 January 1897 and appointed to the Ordnance Committee. It was in this capacity that he met the shipping magnate Sir Charles Cayzer. He married his daughter Gwendoline in 1902. In late 1897 he was invited to become Vice-Admiral Seymour's flag-captain in the *Centurion*, flag-ship of the China Squadron. Chief-of-staff in Seymour's expedition to relieve the siege of the Peking Legation in 1900, he was shot on 21 June and took several months to recover.

Posted to the Admiralty from 1901–02, he returned to sea in HMS *Drake* as senior captain of a cruiser squadron in 1903. He had caught the eye of Admiral Fisher, who had him brought ashore the following year to serve on the committee overseeing the designs that culminated in the *Dreadnought*. Jellicoe became Director of Naval Ordnance in 1905 and hoisted his rear-admiral's flag in 1907 as second-in-command of the Atlantic Fleet. Controller of the Admiralty from 1908–10, his next two years as Acting Vice-Admiral, Atlantic Fleet confirmed Fisher's opinion that Jellicoe was the man to lead the Royal Navy if and when it came to war with Germany.

Jellicoe was unfailingly polite to senior officers and stokers alike. His relations with the lower deck were excellent, not because he was a populist like certain Second World War commanders, but because he was a gentleman in the old-fashioned sense. He was apt to appear unannounced in any part of the *Iron Duke*, see what his people were about and discuss any problems. He reached across the great divides of rank and class with 18th century ease, in contrast to his successor, the haughty patrician David Beatty, whose movements through his flagship were preceded by a file of marines.

Vice-Admiral Sir David Beatty

The dashing commander of the British battle cruisers, David Beatty was a ruggedly handsome, hard-riding fox hunter. Promoted to rear-admiral in 1910 aged 39, he was the youngest man to achieve flag rank since Nelson. He first distinguished himself in command of the gunboats supporting the invasion of Sudan in 1898, and was promoted to commander after only six years as a lieutenant instead of the usual 11 or 12. Executive officer of the battleship *Barfleur* in 1900, he was wounded in the left arm during the fighting at Tientsin, and was one of four commanders specially promoted to captain that November.

Rapid promotion engendered an arrogance in Beatty, notoriously expressed by his turning down command of the second division of the Atlantic Fleet in 1910. He did not want to be based in Gibraltar, but in England. Two years half-pay were followed by Churchill's appointment as First Lord of the Admiralty and Beatty's appointment as his Naval Secretary. When command of the battle cruiser squadron fell vacant in 1913, Churchill promoted Beatty over the heads of more senior candidates and he hoisted his flag in *Lion* on 1 March.

Beatty led the battle cruisers with great panache. Despite his hearty image, Beatty was better informed on the history of the navy than the technocrat Jellicoe, for whom it was a blind spot. Like his chief, he viewed submarines and aircraft as useful auxiliaries, but believed a fleet action would be decided by big guns. He shared Jellicoe's anxieties about U-boat ambushes and himself spotted a non-existent periscope on occasion. One weakness was his appointment of Ralph Seymour as his flag-lieutenant.

Seymour probably owed his appointment to the fact that his sister was the best friend of Winston Churchill's wife. Beatty retained him throughout the war, but would later confide, 'he lost three battles for me'.

Vizeadmiral Reinhard Scheer

'The man with the iron mask', as he was known behind his back when he commanded the cruiser *Gazelle*, Reinhard Scheer was one of von Tirpitz's protégés. Born in September 1863, he joined the navy in 1879 and was promoted Kapitän zur See in 1905. He commanded the battleship *Elsaß* from 1907–09, taking part in exercises off the Canaries in 1908. Promoted Konteradmiral in 1910, he was Director of the General Department of the Navy office from 1911–13, before assuming command of II Geschwader (pre-Dreadnoughts) flying his flag in the *Preußen*. Appointed Vizeadmiral in December 1913, he took charge of III Geschwader, the most modern Dreadnought squadron, in December 1914.

The shrill patriotism of his memoirs testifies to the passion he brought to the job, however farcical his attempts to present Germany as the victim of British aggression. As one of the officers who repaired each summer to von Tirpitz's estate to plot the expansion of the High Sea Fleet, Scheer helped shape the risk fleet strategy he was explicitly to reject after Jutland. Scheer had a considerable reputation by 1914, and was regarded as the ideal successor by the those opposed to von Ingenohl. However, the kaiser refused to hazard his precious ships to the fire-breathing Scheer. It took a year's agitation on Scheer's behalf to make him reconsider.

Scheer's tactical ideas were conventional. He regarded the line of battle as sacrosanct, steaming to Jutland in a single line ahead. He brought the pre-Dreadnoughts of his old squadron with him, possibly because their commander pleaded for their inclusion, probably because he envisaged a suicide role for these obsolete battleships, grimly known to their crews as 'five-minute ships'.

Vizeadmiral Franz Hipper

The German battle cruisers formed the most powerful of the High Sea Fleet's reconnaissance divisions. The 'scouting ships' (*Aufklärungschiffe*) were commanded by a flamboyant Bavarian, Franz Hipper. A trim Van Dyke moustache and beard gave him a buccaneering air. At 53, he was the same age as Scheer, but his career had not taken him to the Navy Office. He joined the torpedo forces in 1893, then served aboard the battleship *Kurfurst Friedrich Wilhelm* from 1898–99. Three years on the royal yacht *Hohenzollern* followed, before he assumed command of II.Torpedoboot abteilung in 1902. In 1906 he took charge of the cruiser *Leipzig* and commanded the heavy cruiser *Friederich Carl*, then *Gneisenau*. He was promoted Kapitän zur See in 1907. He returned to the torpedo boat forces again in 1908, commanding I. Torpedoboote division until he was appointed second-in-command of the scouting forces in 1911. He raised his flag as Konteradmiral in 1912 and became Befehlshaber d. Aufklärungschiffe in 1913.

Promoted Vizeadmiral in June 1915, Hipper had proven himself an enterprising officer during the 'tip-and-run' raids against the English east coast. He resented the inaction that followed his defeat at Dogger Bank and was delighted at the appointment of Scheer.

As one of von Tirpitz's favourites, Admiral Reinhard Scheer had helped plan the High Sea Fleet when he was a junior officer. His efforts to trap an isolated British squadron ended at Jutland when he blundered into the full strength of the Grand Fleet. His subsequent report to the kaiser recognised the futility of a surface action and demanded the resumption of unrestricted U-boat warfare. (IWM)

OPPOSING PLANS

Scheer took the High Sea Fleet to sea in March 1916, and cruised as far as the Texel in the hope of snapping up British light forces. On 24 March, the British launched a seaplane attack against Hoyer, on the Schleswig coast, in the mistaken belief it was a Zeppelin base. Scheer ordered Hipper to put to sea that night, but neither side made contact in the heavy weather. Scheer sortied again on 24 April, the battle cruisers bombarded Lowestoft, covered by his battleships. Light forces clashed, but the Germans steamed for home before the Grand Fleet reached the area. Suspicion that the Germans might essay a cruiser raid into the Channel led the Admiralty to order the 3rd Battle Squadron from Rosyth to Sheerness; the surviving seven pre-Dreadnoughts of the 'Wobbly Eight' (King Edward VII class) were led by *Dreadnought* herself and supported by the 3rd Cruiser Squadron. A proposal to transfer Sturdee's newly created 4th Battle Squadron (the early Dreadnoughts) from Scapa to the Humber was dropped after protests from Jellicoe and Beatty.

On 4 May Jellicoe launched another seaplane attack, this time on the island of Sylt. The raid was covered by the Grand Fleet and minefields were sown in the anticipated path of the High Sea Fleet. British submarines lay in wait too, but Scheer ventured cautiously to Sylt then returned to harbour. The only casualty of the operation was the Zeppelin *L 7*, shot down by the light cruisers *Galatea* and *Phaeton*. Seven survivors were rescued by the British submarine *E 31*.

The outbreak of war caught the Moltke class battle cruiser *Goeben* in the Mediterranean. She evaded a British squadron to reach Constantinople where she notionally joined the Turkish fleet and fought in the Black Sea. The absence of this powerful unit left the German battle cruiser squadron significantly outnumbered in the North Sea. (Author's Collection)

Inflexible picks up survivors from the German armoured cruiser *Gneisenau* after the textbook action off the Falklands on 8 December 1914. Together with *Invincible*, she stayed at long range to pound the German cruisers from beyond effective range of their smaller calibre guns. This was the role for which battle cruisers were conceived. (IWM)

German U-boats were ordered to cease unrestricted attacks after the torpedoing of the *Sussex* brought fierce protest from the United States. Scheer decided to ambush the Grand Fleet with the recalled submarines. Hipper's battle cruisers were ordered to bombard Sunderland and draw out Beatty, while Scheer followed with the High Sea Fleet. A screen of Zeppelins would watch out for Jellicoe. Nineteen U-boats were ordered to sea on 17 May.

Seydlitz was damaged by a mine in April and her repairs took longer than anticipated. A design fault in the König class Dreadnoughts made the consequences of condenser failure particularly serious, so their condensers were overhauled in readiness for the new operation. Scheer delayed putting to sea while repairs continued, but had to sail by 1 June because the U-boats only had an endurance of 20 days. *Seydlitz* was ready by 29 May, but gales ruled out Zeppelin flights and the winds were still too severe on 30 May. Scheer decided to forego aerial reconnaissance and carry out a modified sortie: Hipper would steam up the Danish coast into the Skagerrak where neutral vessels or British intelligence gatherers (the mythical spy trawlers) would report him. Scheer would follow. If the British rose to the bait, their capital ships would pass over Scheer's U-boats and if it came to an action, the Germans would be near their bases and protective minefields.

The British feared the Germans would lay mines in their wake. The Dreadnought *Audacious* succumbed to a single mine in 1914; the disaster was kept secret, but left Jellicoe doubtful about his battleships' underwater protection. During the night action at Tsushima, Japanese destroyers torpedoed the Russian battleship *Navarin*, then finished her off by laying 24 mines in her path, one or two of which exploded with fatal effect. The Grand Fleet included several fast minelayers, one of which was detached at Jutland to mine the Germans' expected route

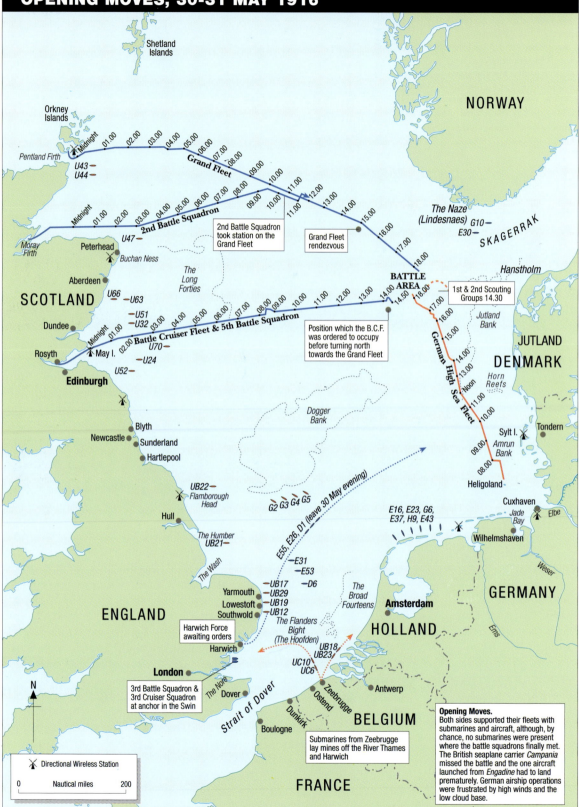

Shetland
Islands

NORWAY

Orkney
Islands

Pentland Firth Midnight 01.00 02.00 03.00 04.00 05.00 06.00 07.00 08.00 09.00 10.00 11.00 12.00 13.00 14.00 15.00 16.00 17.00 18.00

Grand Fleet

U43
U44

The Naze
(Lindesnaes) G10
E30

SKAGERRAK

Midnight 01.00 02.00 03.00 04.00 05.00 06.00 07.00 08.00 09.00 10.00 11.00 12.00 13.00 14.00 15.00

2nd Battle Squadron

Moray
Firth

U47

Peterhead

Buchan Ness

2nd Battle Squadron
took station on the
Grand Fleet

Grand Fleet
rendezvous

Hansholm

Aberdeen

The
Long
Forties

U66 U63

**BATTLE
AREA**

14.00
14.50 18.00

1st & 2nd Scouting
Groups 14.30

17.00
16.00

Jutland
Bank

SCOTLAND

U51
U32

Midnight 01.00 02.00 03.00 04.00 05.00 06.00 07.00 08.00 09.00 10.00 11.00 12.00 13.00 14.00

15.00

JUTLAND

Dundee

May I.

Battle Cruiser Fleet & 5th Battle Squadron

U70

U24

14.00

DENMARK

Rosyth

U52

Position which the B.C.F.
was ordered to occupy
before turning north
towards the Grand Fleet

German High Sea Fleet

13.00
Noon

Horn
Reefs

Edinburgh

Dogger
Bank

11.00
10.00

Sylt I.

Tondern

Blyth

Amrun
Bank

Newcastle
Sunderland

09.00

Hartlepool

08.00

Heligoland

Cuxhaven

UB22
Flamborough
Head

G2 G3 G4 G5

E16, E23, G6,
E37, H9, E43

Jade
Bay

Elbe

Hull

E55, E26, D1 (leave 30 May evening)

Wilhelmshaven

GERMANY

The Humber
UB21

Weser

The Wash

E31

E53 D6

UB17

Yarmouth UB29
Lowestoft UB19
Southwold UB12

The Broad
Fourteens

Amsterdam

ENGLAND

The Flanders
Bight
(The Hoofden)

HOLLAND

Harwich Force
awaiting orders

Harwich

UB18
UB23

UC10
UC6

Ems

London

The Nore

3rd Battle Squadron &
3rd Cruiser Squadron
at anchor in the Swin

Dover

Zeebrugge

Antwerp

N

Strait of Dover

Ostend

BELGIUM

Dunkirk

Boulogne

Submarines from Zeebrugge
lay mines off the River Thames
and Harwich

FRANCE

✠ Directional Wireless Station

0 Nautical miles 200

Opening Moves.
Both sides supported their fleets with
submarines and aircraft, although, by
chance, no submarines were present
where the battle squadrons finally met.
The British seaplane carrier *Campania*
missed the battle and the one aircraft
launched from *Engadine* had to land
prematurely. German airship operations
were frustrated by high winds and the
low cloud base.

home. The British expected the Germans to do the same, and this was another reason why Admiral Jellicoe informed the Admiralty in 1914 that he did not intend to pursue the German battle fleet if he thought he was being drawn into an ambush by submarines and or minelayers.

Three of the German submarines were mine-layers. One was sunk en route by armed trawlers, one returned with an oil leak, but *U 75* laid mines in a channel 2 miles (3 km) west of the Orkneys. This had no effect on Jutland, but on the night of 5 June HMS *Hampshire* struck one of the mines and sank with heavy loss of life, including Lord Kitchener, Secretary of State for War.

By the last days of May the British knew the U-boats were on station: there had been contacts with Royal Navy submarines and light forces off Scapa, Aberdeen and the Forth. Nevertheless, Jellicoe planned a sweep of his own for 1 June; cruisers would penetrate as far as the Skaw with the Grand Fleet in support. The minelayer *Abdiel* was ordered to mine the channel south of the Vyl lightship and the seaplane carrier *Engadine* would be within range of the Horns Reef to engage German airships. Three British submarines were to be off the Vyl lightship and two more east of Dogger Bank.

Preparations were interrupted on 29 May when the Admiralty deciphered Scheer's warning order, transmitted by radio on the 28th. Jellicoe and Beatty were warned that a major German move was imminent, that it would last two days or so, and they were to concentrate in their usual position, the 'Long Forties' 100 miles (161 km) east of Aberdeen.

The order found Admiral Beatty short of battle cruisers. On 22 April *Australia* had collided with *New Zealand* and was sent to Devonport for repairs. Admiral Hood's 3rd BCS was at Scapa for gunnery practice. The Admiralty suspected that the Germans had completed not just the *Lützow*

Gneisenau, seen here, and sistership *Scharnhorst,* were hopelessly outmatched at the battle of the Falklands, but fought to the last under the command of Admiral von Spee. His defeat of a British cruiser squadron off Chile in November 1914 was the first British defeat at sea for 100 years. (IWM)

ORDERS OF BATTLE

THE GRAND FLEET

Organisation as it sailed 30 May 1916.
The Grand Fleet was missing one battleship,
Emperor of India (4th BS) which was refitting.

2nd Battle Squadron
Ajax
Centurion
Erin
King George V FLAGSHIP V.Adm. Jerram

Conqueror
Monarch
Orion FLAGSHIP R.Adm. Leveson
Thunderer

4th Battle Squadron
Iron Duke FLEET FLAGSHIP Admiral Jellicoe
Canada
Royal Oak
Superb FLAGSHIP R.Adm. Duff

Bellerophon
Benbow FLAGSHIP V.Adm.Sturdee
Temeraire
Vanguard

1st Battle Squadron
Agincourt
Hercules
Marlborough FLAGSHIP V.Adm. Sir Cecil
Burney
Revenge

Collingwood
Colossus FLAGSHIP R.Adm. Gaunt
Neptune
St. Vincent

Light cruisers attached to battle fleet
Active
Bellona
Blanche
Boadicea
Canterbury
Chester

3rd Battle Cruiser Squadron
Indomitable
Inflexible
Invincible FLAGSHIP R.Adm. Hood

1st Cruiser Squadron
Black Prince
Defence FLAGSHIP R.Adm. Arbuthnot
Duke of Edinburgh
Warrior

2nd Cruiser Squadron
Cochrane
Hampshire
Minotaur FLAGSHIP R.Adm. Heath
Shannon

4th Light Cruiser Squadron
Calliope Cdre. Le Mesurier
Caroline
Comus
Constance
Royalist

4th Destroyer Flotilla
Acasta
Achates
Ambuscade
Ardent
Broke
Christopher
Contest
Fortune
Garland
Hardy
Midge
Ophelia
Owl
Porpoise
Shark
Sparrowhawk
Spitfire
Tipperary Capt. Wintour
Unity

7th Flotilla
Castor (light cruiser) Cdre. Hawksley
Kempenfelt
Magic
Mandate
Manners
Marne
Martial
Michael
Milbrook
Minion
Moon
Morning Star
Mounsey
Mystic
Ossory

12th Destroyer Flotilla
Faulknor
Maenad Capt. Stirling
Marksman
Marvel
Mary Rose
Menace
Mindful
Mischief
Munster
Narwhal
Nessus
Noble
Nonsuch
Obedient
Onslaught
Opal

Attached
Abdiel (minelayer)
Campania (seaplane carrier)
Oak (destroyer, tender to fleet flagship *Iron Duke*)

THE BATTLE CRUISER FLEET

Lion FLEET FLAGSHIP V.Adm. Beatty

1st Battle Cruiser Squadron
Princess Royal FLAGSHIP R.Adm. Brock
Queen Mary
Tiger

2nd Battle Cruiser Squadron
Indefatigable
New Zealand FLAGSHIP R.Adm. Pakenham

5th Battle Squadron
Barham FLAGSHIP R.Adm. Evan-Thomas
Malaya
Valiant
Warspite

1st Light Cruiser Squadron
Cordelia
Galatea Cdre. Alexander-Sinclair
Inconstant
Phaeton

2nd Light Cruiser Squadron
Birmingham
Dublin
Nottingham
Southampton Cdre. Goodenough

3rd Light Cruiser Squadron
Birkenhead
Falmouth FLAGSHIP R.Adm. Napier
Gloucester
Yarmouth

1st Destroyer Flotilla
Acheron
Ariel
Attack
Badger
Defender
Fearless (light cruiser) Capt. C. D. Roper
Goshawk
Hydra
Lapwing
Lizard

9th/10th Destroyer Flotillas (combined)
Landrail
Laurel
Liberty
Lydiard Cdr. Goldsmith
Moorsom
Morris
Termagent
Turbulent

13th Destroyer Flotilla
Champion (light cruiser) Capt. Farie
Moresby
Narborough
Nerissa
Nestor
Nicator
Nomad
Obdurate
Onslow
Pelican
Petard

Seaplane carrier: *Engadine*

HOCHSEEFLOTTE
Admiral Scheer left the Dreadnought *König Albert* in dockyard hands. Two pre-Dreadnoughts from II Geschwader were unavailable: *Lothringen* was unfit for service and *Preußen* had been detached to C.-in-C. Baltic forces. British intelligence was incorrect: neither the battle cruiser *Hindenburg*, nor the ex-Greek *Salamis*, nor the 15-in. (381 mm) gun *Bayern* were ready for battle. The only important addition to the High Sea Fleet was the battle cruiser *Lützow* to which Hipper transferred his flag.

III Geschwader
Grosser Kurfürst
König FLAGSHIP KAdm. Behncke
Kronprinz
Markgraf

Kaiser FLAGSHIP KAdm. Nordmann
Kaiserin
Prinz-Regent Luitpold

I Geschwader
Friedrich der Große FLEET FLAGSHIP
    VAdm. Scheer
Helgoland
Oldenburg
Ostfriesland FLAGSHIP VAdm. Schmidt
Thüringen

Nassau
Posen FLAGSHIP KAdm. Engelhardt
Rheinland
Westfalen

II Geschwader
Deutschland FLAGSHIP KAdm. Mauve
Pommern
Schliesen

Hannover FLAGSHIP KAdm. von Dalwigk zu
    Lichtenfels
Hessen
Schleswig-Holstein

IV Aufklärungsgruppe
Frauenlob
Hamburg KzS Bauer, Führer des U-boote
München
Stettin KzS von Reuter
Stuttgart

Torpedoboote
Rostock (light cruiser) KzS Michelson, Führer des Torpedoboote

I Flotille
G 38
G 39 KL Albrecht
G 40
S 32

III Flotille
G 42
G 88
S 53 Korvettenkapitän Hollmann
S 54
V 48
V 71
V 73

V Flotille
G11 Korvettenkapitän Heinecke
G 10
G 7
G 8
G 9
V 1
V 2
V 3
V 4
V 5
V 6

VII Flotille
S 15
S 16
S 17
S 18
S 19
S 20
S 23
S 24 Korvettenkapitän von Koch
V 189

AUFKLÄRUNGSCHIFFE

I Aufklärungsgruppe
Derfflinger
Lützow FLAGSHIP VAdm. Hipper
Moltke
Seydlitz
Von der Tann

II Aufklärungsgruppe
Elbing
Frankfurt FLAGSHIP KAdm. Bödicker
Pillau
Wiesbaden

Torpedoboote
Regensburg (light cruiser)
II F.d.T Kommodore Heinrich

II Flotille
B 97
B 98 Fregattenkapitän Schuur
B 109
B 110
B 111
B 112
G 101
G 102
G 103
G 104

VI Flotille
G 37
G 41 Korvettenkapitän Schultz
G 86
G 87
S 50
V 44
V 45
V 46
V 69

IX Flotille
S 33
S 34
S 35
S 36
S 51
S 52
V 26
V 27
V 28 Korvettenkapitän Goehle
V 29
V 30

but also the *Hindenburg*, so Beatty could be outnumbered. Beatty was more than compensated: Rear-Admiral Evan-Thomas and four 15-in. (381 mm) gun Queen Elizabeth class 'fast battleships' were attached to his command. Beatty's reputation led Hood to fear for the consequences, 'If David Beatty has those ships with him, nothing will stop him from taking on the whole German fleet.' Jellicoe shared his anxiety.

The differences between the British and German battle fleets have often been exaggerated. Their technical strengths and weaknesses cancelled each other out. The shooting of the battle squadrons at Jutland was very similar, both sides scoring about 3 percent hits. British examination of German battleships after the war suggested their armour protection failed to meet the metallurgical quality of the British and, ironically, their ammunition handling procedures were regarded as unsafe. Their greater internal subdivision (more watertight compartments) was compromised by a profusion of voicepipes along which flooding could be expected.

U-boat operations in support of the High Sea Fleet involved *U 43* and *U 44* patrolling off the Pentland Firth; *U 66, U 63, U 51, U 32, U 70, U 24, U 52* and *UB 27* lay off the Forth; *U 47* was off Peterhead; *UB 21* and *UB 22* were off the Humber. *U 67* and *U 46* patrolled off Terschelling. All but *U 47* were scheduled to return to Germany on the evening of 1 June.

The day before the High Sea Fleet sortied, several coastal U-boats from the Flanders Flotilla left Zeebrugge: *UC 10* and *UC 6* were to lay mines off Harwich and the Thames; *UB 17, UB 29, UB 19, UB 12, UB 10* and *UB 6* were to patrol off the Suffolk coast until the afternoon of 2 June. *UB 23* and *UB 18* were to patrol Terschelling.

The Admiralty kept back the 3rd Battle Squadron at Sheerness and the Harwich Force (four light cruisers and 34 destroyers) until German movements became clearer. However, there were some two dozen British submarines based at Harwich and Blyth of which *E 16, E 23, E 37, G 6, E 43* and *H 9* were patrolling Terschelling, two made unsuccessful torpedo attacks on U-boats. They were due to return on 1 June. *D 3, H 10* and *V 1* left Harwich to replace them at noon on 1 June. The destroyer *Lurcher* sailed from Harwich on the evening of 30 May, with *E 31, E 53*

Germany's last and most powerful armoured cruiser, *Blücher*, remained with Hipper's battle cruiser squadron despite her much inferior armament. At the tail of his line during the Dogger Bank action in 1915, she lost power after several hits and was overhauled and sunk. But for a series of British signalling errors, the rest of the squadron might have joined her. (Author's Collection)

The High Sea Fleet banned the use of cameras at sea, but several British officers took photographs at the battles of the Falklands, Dogger Bank and Jutland. Given the circumstances and the nature of the equipment, it is unsurprising that their resolution is not great. However, they give a vital glimpse of the action. Here the British battle cruisers come under fire from Hipper's squadron during the 'run to the south' at Jutland. (IWM)

and *D 6* to patrol towards the Dutch coast. *E 55*, *E 26*, and *D 1* departed Harwich on 30 May to take up station of the Vyl lightship; *G 2*, *G 3*, *G 4* and *G 5* escorted by the destroyer *Talisman* left Blyth on 31 May bound for the Dogger Bank. *E 30* and *G 10* lay off southern Norway.

The Germans broadcast their change of plan to their U-boats in the North Sea, but only four received the orders and only one, *U 32* managed to engage. At 0400hrs on 31 May she fired torpedoes at the 1st Light Cruiser Squadron but had to dive to avoid being rammed by HMS *Phaeton*. *U 66* observed the 2nd Battle Squadron some 60 miles (97 km) east of Peterhead and transmitted a sighting report. The great U-boat ambush failed. Although there were 13 reported sightings of U-boats in the Grand Fleet at Jutland, none were in the battle area. Reports from *U 32* and *U 66* left Scheer optimistic: several British squadrons appeared to be out, there was no evidence they were combining against him. Perhaps he could succeed where Ingenohl had failed.

Scheer received belated support from the Zeppelins. In the late forenoon of 31 May the wind had abated sufficiently for *L 9*, *L 14*, *L 16*, *L 21* and *L 23* to go up. Scouting from the Skagerrak to Flamborough Head, they discovered that the cloud base was little more than 328 yards (300 m); visibility was poor even when the hazy conditions permitted a view of the sea.

The departure of the squadrons was accompanied by a disastrous error in the British signals intelligence operation. The Admiralty's Director of Operations, Admiral Jackson, asked Room 40 where they placed the German call sign 'DK'. The answer was Wilhelmshaven, but it was the wrong question. DK was Scheer's call sign, but only in harbour; when he put to sea, he used 'RÄ'. Thus Jackson would later signal Jellicoe that the German High Sea Fleet was in harbour.

One other error marred the British deployment. The seaplane carrier *Campania* missed the order to sail, but put to sea the following morning, determined to catch up. When Jellicoe was informed, he ordered her to return rather than brave the German submarine lines alone. Whether her aircraft or captive balloon would have influenced the outcome is one of Jutland's many 'what ifs?'

THE BATTLE

'Enemy in sight'

Vizeadmiral Hipper led the German battle cruisers out of the Jade Basin at 0100hrs on 31 May. Scheer followed at 0130hrs. II Geschwader sailed from the Elbe and joined the Dreadnoughts three hours later. The battleships were in single line ahead, steaming at 14 knots at intervals of 766 yards (700 m); a 2.2-mile (3.5 km) gap was maintained between the squadrons. A clear night gave way to a beautiful sunrise, visibility was excellent and for some hours the two squadrons remained in sight. Hipper's squadron made 16 knots and at length the battle squadrons vanished astern. There was speculation over lunch that they might encounter British cruisers reported off Norway; in the afternoon the battle cruisers carried out gunnery drill and cleaned the guns. Having changed the elements on the hit indicators, the gunnery officer of *Derfflinger*, Korvettenkapitän Georg von Hase, settled down in the wardroom for a smoke and a cup of coffee. It was 1428hrs.

Beatty and Hipper had been on a collision course since the morning. Yet, had a chance encounter with a neutral vessel not attracted the attention of their cruisers, they would not have met until at least an hour later, and a daylight action between the battle fleets would have been unlikely. The Danish tramp steamer *N.J. Fjord* was sighted by the *Elbing* at 1400hrs and two torpedo boats, *B 109* and *B 110* steered westwards to examine her. Simultaneously, the *Galatea* and *Phaeton* turned east to investigate. *Inconstant* and *Cordelia* followed, and at 1420hrs saw the signal they had all been waiting for break out from *Galatea*'s masthead: 'ENEMY IN SIGHT'. *Galatea* also signalled by radio: 'URGENT TWO CRUISERS, PROBABLY HOSTILE, IN SIGHT. BEARING ESE, COURSE UNKNOWN, MY POSITION

The third class of German Dreadnoughts, the Kaisers, adopted super-firing turrets aft with the midships turrets offset to give limited cross-deck firing arcs. *Kaiserin* escaped with little damage at Jutland. Sistership *Friederich der Große* was Admiral Scheer's flagship. (IWM)

38

Birmingham barely visible among shell splashes as the light cruisers come under fire from the battleships of the High Sea Fleet. (IWM)

OVERLEAF *Lion* leads the pack. At 1548hrs, the Germans opened fire. Beatty's flagship engaged *Lützow,* the flagship of Vizeadmiral Hipper. The German ships fired regularly and accurately, hitting *Lion, Princess Royal* and *Tiger* in the first minutes of the engagement. A shell from *Lützow* destroyed part of the roof of 'Q' turret on *Lion,* igniting cordite charges, and producing an explosion and fire which killed 70 men.

LAT 56° 48' N, LONG 5°, 21' E.' Telegraphists all over the Grand Fleet picked up the message.

Recognition was mutual. The torpedo boats fell back on their cruisers, shell splashes soaring around them as *Galatea* and *Phaeton* opened fire. *Elbing* reported them as armoured cruisers, then the British turned north to engage broadside to broadside, and *Elbing* opened fire at 14,000 yards (12,740 m), striking *Galatea* with a 5.9 in (150 mm) shell that failed to explode. Since British signalling errors will loom large in the following story, it is worth noting the alarm triggered by *Elbing*'s next signal. She observed the recognition signal flashed by the British ('PL') and signalled it to *Frankfurt* and *Lützow,* but her searchlight signal was read as 'HAVE SIGHTED 24 TO 26 BATTLESHIPS'! This was soon corrected to 'FOUR LIGHT CRUISERS'. Hipper led his battle cruisers in pursuit, working up to 23 knots.

Von Hase had barely sat down when there was a thunder of drums and whistles and shouts of 'Clear for Action!' No one could believe it. Aboard the *New Zealand* news that the enemy had been sighted 'was received in the ward-room with cold suspicion' according to one of her gunnery officers, and 'although one or two officers came on deck to have a look round, the general attitude was one of scepticism. Then came a report of a large amount of smoke, probably of a fleet bearing east-north-east and we started to "sit up and take notice". Action stations were sounded, and as I climbed on to the rungs of the mast to go aloft, a sailor asked breathlessly if the Huns were in sight, and I told him they were. All turrets and stations were reported cleared away and correct in record time.'[4] At 1500hrs Jellicoe hoisted the signal 'BJ': 'ASSUME COMPLETE READINESS FOR ACTION IN EVERY RESPECT'. On every ship, great and small, men mustered at their stations; gas masks, goggles and life-belts appeared; splinter mats, fire hoses, boxes of sand, stretchers, shoring-up spars, spare electrical equipment, spare hydraulic gear...the drills were familiar, faster this day as the news spread that the enemy were present.

British ships had been ordered to fly a Union flag at the mainmast in addition to the White Ensign because the latter could be confused with

39

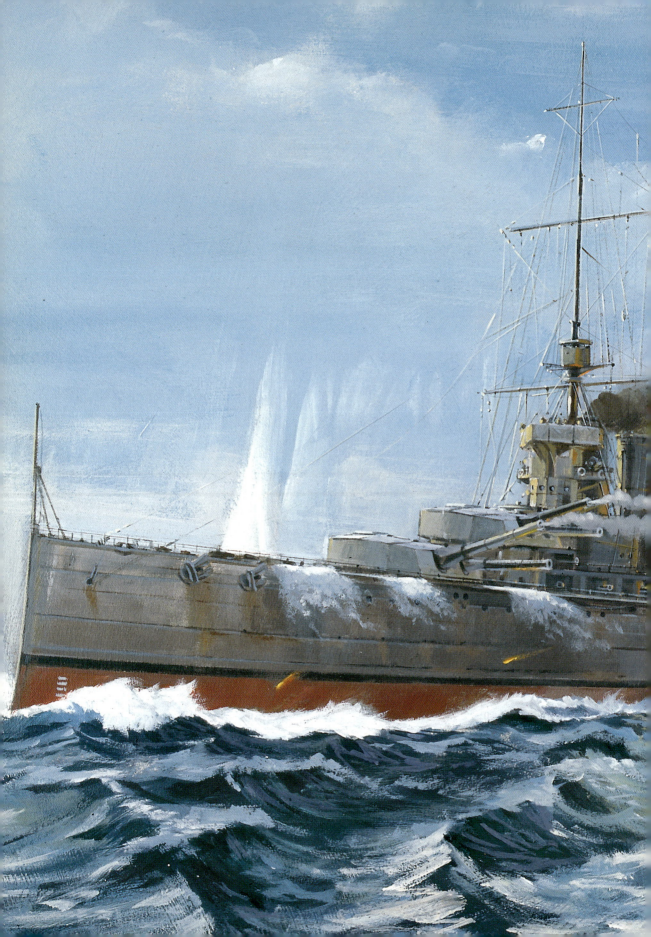

the German naval ensign. As Jellicoe's Dreadnoughts surged forward with new purpose, great battle-ensigns broke out on yardarms throughout the fleet. A midshipman on the *Neptune* saw battleships with three or four battle-ensigns streaming defiantly in the wind.

Beatty sensed the chance of cutting off the German force and ordered his squadrons to steer south-south-east. The signal was made by flags and he did not wait for it to be acknowledged before hauling it down, making it executive. This was in accordance with his standing orders, instructions that Evan-Thomas and the 5th Battle Squadron had never read. The flags were seen from *Barham* but were not identifiable. Since the squadron was due to turn on the next leg of its zig-zag course, it was assumed to be the expected order to turn two points to port. Beatty's battle cruisers steered SSE, increasing speed while the 5th Battle Squadron turned north-by-west.

Evan-Thomas maintained this reciprocal course, placidly watching the battle cruisers until they vanished into the haze created by their own funnel smoke. What he thought he was doing is anyone's guess; the incident does not appear in his account of the battle, the official history or even Professor Marder's account.[5] By the time it dawned on him to go after Beatty he was as much as 10 miles (16 km) behind. 'The result, however, of his eight minutes' delay in turning was inexorably to keep him and his tremendous guns out of the action for the first most critical and most fatal half-hour, and even thereafter to keep him at extreme range.'[6]

Beatty forged ahead, attention focused on the distant enemy. *Galatea* reported the presence of heavy smoke along the horizon. Beatty ordered the *Engadine* to send up one of her floatplanes. In record time, the Short 184 was taxiing across the water with Flight Officer Frederick Rutland at the controls and Assistant Paymaster G. S. Trewin acting as observer. The cloud base was at about 1,000 feet (303 m), which, as Rutland observed, 'necessitated flying very low. On sighting the enemy it was very hard to tell what they were, and so I had to close to within a mile and a half at a height of 1,000 feet. They [Bödicker's light cruisers] then opened fire on

The Short 184 Seaplane was one of several types employed by the Royal Navy Air Service. 'Rutland of Jutland', as he became known, piloted a 184 on a brief sortie during the afternoon of 31 May, but was forced down by engine failure. His report failed to reach Admiral Jellicoe and the battle was fought without benefit of aerial reconnaissance. (IWM)

me with anti-aircraft and other guns, my height enabling them to use their anti-torpedo armament'[7]. Trewin reported that the Germans were jamming his transmissions, and the flight was cut short at 1545hrs when a fuel pipe broke. Although Rutland managed to repair it, he was hoisted in at 1600hrs His messages were received in *Engadine* but she did not succeed in passing them on. The increasing swell ruled out another flight and the battle would be conducted without aerial reconnaissance.

The battle cruiser fleets sighted each other just after 1520hrs. Bugles sounded action stations, but some officers and men on both sides assumed it was another drill. They soon discovered otherwise. Korvetttenkapitän von Hase of the *Derfflinger* reported that 'There was still no sign of the enemy. Nevertheless, we could see a change in the situation: the light cruisers and destroyers turned about and were taking shelter behind the battle cruisers. Thus we were at the head of the line. The horizon ahead of us grew clear of smoke, and we could make out some English light cruisers which had also turned about. Suddenly my periscope revealed some big ships. Black monsters; six tall, broad-beamed giants steaming in two columns. They were still a long way

Rearmost ship in Hipper's squadron, *Von der Tann* engaged *Indefatigable*, her opposite number in Beatty's line. In 15 minutes of fast and accurate shooting, she scored half-a-dozen hits, one of which exploded *Indefatigable*'s magazine. (IWM)

LEFT AND MIDDLE **Beatty's flagship *Lion* engaging Hipper's battle cruisers.**

BOTTOM **Notice the pall of smoke above 'Q' turret. Mortally wounded, Major Harvey RM won a posthumous Victoria Cross for ordering the magazine flooded as the turret crew perished in the flames as ammunition in the turret caught fire. (IWM)**

off, but they showed up clearly on the horizon, and even at this great distance they looked powerful, massive.'[8]

Beatty directed the 2nd BCS to take station astern of 1st BCS: six British battle cruisers steamed east-south-east with five German battle cruisers steering an almost parallel course, edging to the south-east as Hipper sought to hurry through the 9–11 nautical mile (18–22 km) range band. At this distance it was theoretically possible for the Lion class battle cruisers to engage their lighter-gunned opponents with impunity. In reality, the British over-estimated the range, their gunnery officers muttering darkly as 9th Destroyer Flotilla steamed at full pelt along the engaged side to take station ahead. The German ships were hard to pick out against the grey horizon and the smoky trail left by the destroyers compounded the problem. By contrast, the British were sharply silhouetted by the bright sky in the west.

Hipper gave the order to open fire at 1548hrs. His gunnery officer estimated the range at 8 nautical miles (15.4 km). Beatty's ships fired back 30 seconds later, *Lion* and *Princess Royal* concentrating on *Lützow*, while the following ships engaged their opposite numbers. *Queen Mary* fired on *Seydlitz* when she should have dealt with *Derfflinger*. To the delight of her gunnery officer, the latter was left undisturbed by British fire. *Tiger* did not take in the signal either and joined *New Zealand* against the *Moltke*. The rearmost battle cruisers, *Von der Tann* and *Indefatigable*, embarked on a solitary but deadly duel. Evan-Thomas' four 15-in. (381 mm) gun battleships were now trailing some 7 miles (11 km) astern.

Hipper's battle cruisers had better rangefinders and they were not steaming as fast as the British – Hipper slowed to 18 knots to allow his cruisers to catch up. Engaging from windward further handicapped the British: voluminous clouds of propellent gases discharged from the great guns followed the path of the shells towards the enemy, along with thick coils of funnel smoke. The Germans fired with clockwork regularity, four-gun salvoes every 20 seconds. In the first few minutes, *Lion*, *Princess Royal* and *Tiger* were all hit; *Princess Royal*'s fore turret was knocked out, *Tiger* lost 'Q' and 'X' turrets. The opening British salvoes landed a mile beyond the Germans.

The battle lines converged. Just before 1600hrs, the range fell to below 6.3 nautical miles (11.8 km) and some of the Germans opened fire with their 5.9-in (150 mm) guns too, One observer remembered, 'after each salvo of the heavy guns the secondary armament was to fire two salvoes in quick succession and henceforward fire in conjunction with the heavy guns. Then began an ear-splitting, stupefying din. Including the secondary armament we were firing on an average one mighty salvo every seven seconds…While the firing was going on any observation was out of the question. Dense masses of smoke accumulated round the muzzles of the guns, growing into clouds as high as houses…we could see nothing of the enemy for seconds at a time as our fore-control was completely enveloped in smoke'.[9]

KzS von Egidy of the *Seydlitz* was informed by his gunnery control station that 'C' turret was not responding. Smoke poured from the voice pipes. A 13.5-in. (323 mm) shell from *Queen Mary* had exploded as it penetrated the barbette, igniting four charges and burning to death every man in the handling room and most of the turret crew. But the restrictions he had imposed after the Dogger Bank action, limiting the

number of charges allowed in the turret, paid off: the fire did not spread to the magazine and the crew there survived by donning gas masks.

Both sides altered course to open the range. As they did, *Lion* took another hit, a 12-in. (305 mm) shell from *Lützow* blowing off part of the roof of 'Q' turret. Cordite charges in the loading cages about to enter the guns, ignited with terrible effect, killing almost everyone in the gun house. The turret commander, Major F. J. W. Harvey, was mortally wounded but managed to give the order to flood the magazines, for which he was awarded a posthumous Victoria Cross. Somehow, the flames were extinguished, but minutes later, smouldering charges caught fire and a second explosion occurred, flames shot up as high as the masthead and 70 men of the magazine and shell room crews were burned to death. Had the magazine not been already flooded, *Lion* would have blown up too.[10]

Lieutenant W. S. Chalmers was on *Lion*'s bridge, where the hum of shell fragments marked each hit on his ship. 'We hoped the enemy was being similarly punished but the five shadowy forms, with sporadic tongues of fire leaping from their guns, were apparently none the worse and we could not tell what damage we were doing to them as it was difficult to see the splashes of our shells in the white mist. At about this time a bloodstained Sergeant of Marines appeared on the bridge. He was hatless, his clothes were burnt and he seemed somewhat dazed. I asked him what was the matter; in a tired voice he replied: "Q turret has gone, sir. All the crew are killed, and we have flooded the magazine".'[11]

Beatty's destroyers were now concentrated ahead of his line, poised to attack. Beatty ordered a torpedo attack just after 1600hrs, but *Lion*'s radio was damaged and the signal was passed by flags via *Princess Royal*. Crucially, the order was not taken in by the flotillas for another ten minutes.

The action between *Von der Tann* and *Indefatigable* lasted just a quarter of an hour. At 1603hrs gunnery officer Korvettenkapitän Marholz observed hits from two successive salvoes. Observers in *New Zealand*'s conning tower saw that *Indefatigable* had been hit abaft her mainmast; smoke billowed from her superstructure. She failed to follow

New Zealand in a turn to port, and held on until she was 500 yards (455 m) off her starboard quarter, settling by the stern and listing to port. Shells from the second salvo hit her on the forecastle and 'A' turret. Thirty seconds later, she exploded with incredible force, a 50-ft (15 m) steam picket boat soaring 200 feet (60 m) into the air. 1,017 officers and men went down with her. Two survivors were picked up by the German torpedo boat *S 16* after some four hours in the water.

By this time Evan-Thomas had the battle cruisers in sight. *Barham* opened fire on *Von der Tann* at 11 miles (17 km). Beatty had turned away after a succession of torpedo reports and the alleged sighting of a periscope. (In fact, the *Moltke* had launched torpedoes at *Queen Mary* as the range approached 10,000 yards (910 m), but the British sighted torpedo tracks on their disengaged side.) *Von der Tann* suffered a serious hit, and only very quick work by her damage-control teams prevented a machinery breakdown that would have left her helpless in the path of the oncoming battleships. Her 'A' turret was struck and the training gear jammed. *Moltke*'s 5.9-in. (150 mm) battery was penetrated by a 15-in. (381 mm) shell that set fire to the ammunition in one casemate.

Queen Mary engaged *Derfflinger* and *Seydlitz*, the Germans firing four-gun salvoes; *Queen Mary* firing full eight-gun salvoes at *Derfflinger*. At 1625hrs *Queen Mary* was blown in half by the detonation of her midships magazine. Debris soared hundreds of feet into the air to rain down on her next astern, *Tiger*. Petty Officer (Gunner's Mate) E. Francis was one of only eight survivors from the 1,274 officers and men aboard. He was in the aft 13.5-in. (343 mm) turret when a tremendous explosion threw everyone to the floor. The left gun fell through its trunnions, crushing several men beneath it. The ship listed violently to port. Turret commander Lieutenant Ewart gave the order to clear the turret. 'P.O. Stares was the last I saw coming up from the working chamber and I asked whether he had passed the order to the magazine and shell room, and he told me it was no use, as the water was right up the trunk leading from the shell room, so the bottom of the ship must have been out of her.' Petty Officer Francis and a handful of men made it into the water as the stern sank.

Viewed from *Lion*'s bridge, the situation was disastrous. *Indefatigable* and *Queen Mary* had been blown to pieces, leaving the British with four battle cruisers against five. *Lion* was on fire. Then *Princess Royal* vanished from sight in a cloud of smoke and spray as a German salvo struck the sea around her. A signalman leapt to *Lion*'s bridge and reported, '*Princess Royal* blown up, sir'. Vice-Admiral Beatty turned to his flag-captain and said, 'Chatfield, there seems to be something wrong with our bloody ships today.'

While Beatty demonstrated exemplary sang froid, the British destroyers launched their attack. The German torpedo boat commander, Kommodore Heinrich (flying his broad pennant in the cruiser *Regensburg*) had issued similar orders, anticipated by Korvettenkapitän Goehle of IX Torpedoboote Flotille. Ten German boats

At 1625 hrs *Queen Mary* was blown in half by the detonation of her midships magazine. A moment later *Princess Royal* vanished from sight as a German salvo struck the sea around her. (IWM)

II. Aufklärungsgruppe (Konteradmiral Bödicker) *Frankfurt, Pillau, Elbing,* and *Wiesbaden.*

1st and 3rd Light Cruiser Squadrons (*Falmouth, Yarmouth, Birkenhead, Gloucester, Galatea, Phaeton, Inconstant* and *Cordelia*).

N

Indefatigable was the first major casualty, sunk by *Von der Tann* in 15 minutes. Over 1,000 men were killed; two survivors were rescued by the German torpedo boat *S 16* some four hours later.

LIGHT WIND

5th Battle Squadron trailed 10 miles astern before it dawned on Evan-Thomas in *Barham* that he should follow Beatty. At emergency full speed, the Queen Elizabeth class could just reach 24 knots. *Barham* leads *Valiant, Warspite* and *Malaya.*

THE RUN TO THE SOUTH 1610 – 1630HRS

The chance meeting of the British and German battle cruisers was followed by 'the run to the south', as Hipper sought to draw Beatty on to the guns of the High Sea Fleet. British signalling errors led to the powerful 5th Battle Squadron trailing far astern of Beatty's battle cruisers. A deadly combination of bad light, higher speed, wind direction and lack of training meant that the British ships shot far less accurately than their German opponents.

1620HRS: German battle cruisers form line ahead. *Lützow* is followed by *Derfflinger*, *Seydlitz*, *Moltke* and *Von der Tann*; they turned away together at about 1630hrs when the torpedo boats attacked.

1630HRS: *Regensburg*, flying the broad pennant of Kommodore Heinrich, II Führer der Torpedoboote, leads IX Flotille and part of II Flotille to make a torpedo attack.

1630HRS: British 13th Destroyer Flotilla attacks at the same time as the German torpedo boats. In a close range mêlée *Nomad* is disabled, *V 27* and *V 29* are sunk.

1620HRS: **position of 1st and 2nd Battle Cruiser Squadrons. Beatty's flagship *Lion* leads *Princess Royal*, *Queen Mary*, *Tiger* and *New Zealand*.**

2nd Light Cruiser Squadron (Commodore Goodenough): *Southampton*, *Birmingham*, *Nottingham* and *Dublin*.

1626HRS: *Queen Mary* blows up; seconds later *Princess Royal* vanishes behind towering shell splashes.

cut across the bows of *Lützow* as some 13 British destroyers sallied forth. The heavy ships of both sides opened up with their secondary batteries and a high-speed mêlée took place. *Nomad* was disabled by a shell in her engine room from *S 51; V 27* suffered a similar hit and was scuttled, the crew rescued by *V 26. V 29* was torpedoed and left sinking by the stern; she managed to fire torpedoes at the British battleships before she went down.

At 1630hrs Commodore Goodenough, leading the 4th Light Cruiser Squadron in the *Southampton* several miles ahead of *Lion*, sighted a German cruiser in the distance. Closer observation revealed tell-tale plumes of smoke. At 1638hrs she signalled by radio to both Beatty and Jellicoe, 'HAVE SIGHTED ENEMY BATTLE FLEET'. A similar signal from *Champion* confirmed the news.

Jellicoe had detached Hood's 3rd BCS to support Beatty at 1605hrs and the Grand Fleet had accelerated to 20 knots, the maximum it could sustain in cruising formation. But he was taken aback by the news that Scheer's whole fleet was out, that the Admiralty appreciation was completely wrong.

Beatty saw them too. At 1640hrs he ordered his destroyers to fall back and signalled a 16-point turn in succession to starboard. His mission now was to draw the Germans on to the Grand Fleet. British destroyers continued to attack as Hipper swung his big ships through 16 points to follow Beatty. *Von der Tann* was attacked by *Nerissa* and *Termagent* without success; *Petard* missed *Derfflinger* with a spread of three torpedoes, but *Turbulent* hit *Seydlitz* despite some sharp turns ordered by her captain. There was little noise but a rattling in the rigging; for the damage control team, it was a repeat performance of their work after the mine damage five weeks earlier. The torpedo bulkhead held. Where rivets were blown out, the water was kept out by wooden plugs, but many were dislodged just enough to leak. A new contest began, between *Seydlitz*'s pumps and the sea.

Beatty's report was sent via *Princess Royal* and was not taken in by Jellicoe's flagship, but by *Benbow* which passed it on. Somewhere in this game of 'Chinese whispers' the signal 'ENEMY BATTLE FLEET BEARING SE' transmuted into '26–30 BATTLESHIPS...BEARING SSE STEERING E'. To Jellicoe, it confirmed intelligence reports that the Germans were at sea with all 18 Dreadnoughts and up to a dozen pre-Dreadnoughts. His numerical advantage looked less significant. And, since he never saw more than four or five enemy battleships during the whole engagement, he never learned Scheer's true strength until after the battle.

Beatty gave his position, but his dead reckoning was out. So was that of his light cruiser squadron. When examining any map of the battle of Jutland, it is vital to remember that most participants could not tell where they were to any degree of accuracy so forces tended to appear by surprise from unexpected directions. Errors were there from the start: *Galatea*'s first sighting report gave her position several miles south of her actual location; in Hipper's first radio signal to Scheer, he reported himself 10 miles (16 km) south of his true position.

Scheer's battle line shook out into an echeloned formation and the fast König class battleships of his van surged ahead, opening fire on the British battle cruisers at 1646hrs The range was extreme: 12 miles (19 km), but the crippled destroyer *Nestor* was blown to pieces by the

Dreadnoughts' secondary armament. *Kaiser, Friedrich der Große* and the whole I Geschwader fired on Goodenough's light cruisers as they chased the shell splashes, steering towards the last shell bursts. To their astonishment, they escaped without damage.

Beatty's squadron steered almost directly for the 5th Battle Squadron, which continued to fire on Hipper's battle cruisers. Beatty ordered a further four-point turn to starboard so that the battleships would pass on his disengaged side: he would mask the fire of the 15-in. (381 mm) gun battleships, but it was not his style to take shelter behind anyone. Evan-Thomas altered course to starboard too, the two squadrons passing about two miles apart, red-to-red. A few minutes before the two British squadrons passed each other, Beatty signalled to Evan-Thomas 'ALTER COURSE IN SUCCESSION 16 POINTS TO STARBOARD'.

Something went wrong.[13] *Lion*'s signalling staff were dealing with half-a-dozen flag signals as they rushed past the 5th Battle Squadron and this, the most important signal, was not hauled down, i.e. made executive, for several minutes. The 5th Battle Squadron stood on towards the High Seas Fleet instead of forming on the rear of the battle cruisers. Every minute brought Britain's four most powerful battleships another 1,000 yards (910 m) closer to the guns of the High Sea Fleet. Evan-Thomas should have taken station astern of the battle cruisers, but he was frozen into indecision by the sight of that signal, still hoisted. When at length, his squadron did turn, it came under heavy fire from the leading German Dreadnoughts. *Warspite*'s executive officer saw 'masts, funnels and an endless ripple of orange flashes all down the line, how many I didn't try to count as we were getting well strafed, but I remember counting up to eight'. Had any of the Queen Elizabeths been disabled, they would have been left in the path of the High Sea Fleet and destroyed.

For the next 30 minutes, the 5th Battle Squadron steamed north at its top speed of 23–4 knots while the König class exceeded their designed speed and almost maintained the range. Evan-Thomas' ships exchanged shots with III Geschwader and Hipper's battle cruisers. Beatty, signalled Evan-Thomas to take station astern, but maintained at least 25 knots and drew away into the murk. Beatty had to get ahead of the German battle cruisers and drive them eastwards, to prevent Hipper observing the approach of the Grand Fleet until it was too late.

The light cruiser *Regensburg* wore the broad pennant of Kommodore Heinrich, commander of Hipper's torpedo boats. He ordered a torpedo attack on Beatty's battle cruisers at 1630hrs, just as the British destroyers launched a sally of their own. The result was a wild mêlée between the opposing battle cruiser lines. (IWM)

'Fleet action is imminent'

At 1700hrs on 31 May, the Admiralty took in a four-word signal from *Iron Duke* that put an end to normal business: 'FLEET ACTION IS IMMINENT'.

But where and when?

Beatty lost sight of the High Sea Fleet at about 1700hrs and was out of touch with Hipper too from 1715hrs to about 1740hrs, although the battle cruisers could see the 5th Battle Squadron in action. Beatty did not elaborate on his report to Jellicoe at 1645hrs, received in garbled form after transmission via *Princess Royal*. Presumably, he assumed the forces in closer touch with the enemy would report to Jellicoe. That was certainly what Jellicoe expected to happen.

Wondering what had become of his most powerful battle squadron, Jellicoe signalled Evan-Thomas at 1617hrs, asking 'ARE YOU WITH S.O. BATTLE CRUISERS?' to which he received the reply, 'YES I AM ENGAGING THE ENEMY'. An hour later, with Beatty out of sight, Evan-Thomas was the senior British officer in contact with the enemy. Evan-Thomas was the signals guru of the pre-war navy, the apostle of the complex signalling process developed at the turn of the century. It was he who had recommended the introduction of radios to the Royal Navy. The wireless aboard his flagship *Barham* had been shattered, but all three of his other battleships had serviceable radios. Yet no one thought to use them, no one informed Jellicoe what was happening, and he was left to guess what lay ahead.

Admiral Scheer signalled 'GENERAL CHASE' as the 5th Battle Squadron went about. Hipper headed north-west where he ran into Beatty and the 5th Battle Squadron in visibility conditions that favoured the British. By 1800hrs Hipper fell back eastwards, his ships badly damaged. His flagship *Lützow* was shipping large quantities of water although her armament was intact. *Derfflinger* was sinking by the head, the forepart of the ship abandoned.

Seydlitz listed to port and KzS von Egidy had to counter-flood. Concussion from heavy hits played havoc with the electrical system and many compartments were plunged into darkness for long periods. Von Egidy was thankful that he had run so many 'blind man's bluff' exercises in which the crew learned to handle valves and other equipment by touch alone. He singled out his stokers and coal trimmers for special praise: they shovelled away in darkness, up to their knees in water, not knowing if this was the prelude to catastrophic flooding. Only thin beams of torchlight and the glare of the furnaces illuminated the proceedings. The poor quality of German coal choked the fires with slag and it was not possible to clean them quickly enough: the grates burned through and fell into the ash pits. The demand for continued high-speed steaming left the replacement grates melting in the heat by nightfall.

Von der Tann had taken some hard knocks too: she could maintain speed but all eight 11-in. (280 mm) guns were disabled by hits or malfunctions. Only *Moltke* was relatively unscathed.

At 1510hrs Jellicoe had ordered Admirals Arbuthnot and Heath to deploy their armoured cruisers in a screen 16 miles (26 km) ahead of the Grand Fleet. Unfortunately, they never had the margin of speed to get sufficiently far in front. At 1630hrs *Black Prince* spotted Beatty's battle cruisers, but mistook them for Germans. Commodore Goodenough sent off three sighting reports before 1700hrs, but fell silent as the crisis

The foredeck of *Birmingham* showing her 6-in. (150 mm) guns. Part of Commodore Goodenough's 1st Light Cruiser Squadron, accompanying the Battle Cruiser Fleet, she was in the thick of the action from the start. She also took part in the night action with IV Aufklärungsgruppe, during which the German light cruiser *Fraenlob* was torpedoed and sunk. (IWM)

approached. Not until 1750hrs did he signal Jellicoe again, this time to report that the German battle cruisers were now south-west of their battle fleet. They were actually north-east: he had given a reciprocal bearing by mistake. Then the battleship *Marlborough*, leading the starboard wing column reported to Jellicoe that she could see gun flashes ahead. Despairing of anything useful from his cruisers, Jellicoe signalled *Marlborough*, 'WHAT CAN YOU SEE?'

'OUR BATTLE CRUISERS BEARING SOUTH-SOUTH-WEST, STEERING EAST *LION* LEADING SHIP', came the reply, followed by, '5TH BATTLE SQUADRON BEARING SOUTH-SOUTH-WEST'.

This confirmed what Jellicoe suspected: that the dead reckoning errors of the battle cruisers and the Grand Fleet had multiplied. *Lion* was some 11 miles (18 km) east of her position plotted on *Iron Duke*'s chart: the German fleet would be in sight 20 minutes earlier than predicted. At 1756hrs Beatty hove into view, steaming at full speed across the front of the battle fleet, big guns thundering away at targets invisible in the mist,

The Royal Navy's qualitative and quantitative advantage grew during the war. The four 15-in. (381 mm) gun Revenge class battleships entered service 1916–17, three fighting at Jutland. Slower than the Queen Elizabeth class because they reverted to coal-firing, their anti-torpedo bulging gave them a reputation for rolling. *Royal Oak* was sunk at Scapa by *U 47* in 1939. (Author's Collection)

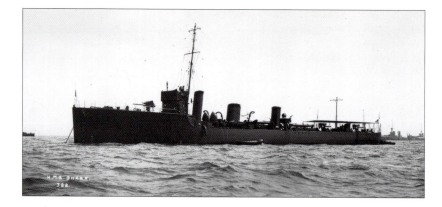

The destroyer *Shark* was disabled by gunfire from the cruiser *Regensburg* and a torpedo from *G 41*. Her commander, Loftus-Jones, was awarded a posthumous Victoria Cross for continuing the fight to the last torpedo despite losing his leg.

If Jellicoe deployed to starboard, he would be in action sooner, but with his oldest Dreadnoughts in the van. Deployment to port might enable him to interpose his battle line between the High Sea Fleet and its base. It would leave the Germans silhouetted by the setting sun that broke through the haze from time to time; he might be able to 'cross the Germans' T'. Yet it would delay the action and it was already after 1800hrs. Historians have weighed his choices since. John Jellicoe had about ten minutes. In his own words, 'At this stage there was still great uncertainty as to the position of the enemy's Battle Fleet; flashes of gunfire were visible from ahead round to the starboard beam, and the noise was heavy and continuous.'[14] At 1815hrs Jellicoe ordered the Grand Fleet to deploy on the port column, south-east-by-east.

Scheer's appreciation of the situation was hindered by the sudden emergence of a new threat from the north-east. At 1612hrs Admiral Hood had gone to full speed to reach Beatty, but errors in dead reckoning meant he passed nearly 20 miles (32 km) east of his chief. He stationed the light cruiser *Chester* 5 miles (8 km) on his starboard beam, *Canterbury* 5 miles (8 km) ahead and four destroyers in front of the battle cruisers as an anti-submarine screen. *Chester* found visibility varying from 1 mile (1.6 km) in some directions to 6–7 miles (9.6–11.3 km) in others. At 1730hrs a three-funnel cruiser could be made out, with torpedo boats in company: this did not look like Beatty's accompanying flotillas. Moments later, she was under fire from Bödicker's light cruiser squadron, *Frankfurt*, *Pillau*, *Elbing* and *Wiesbaden*. HMS *Chester* had several guns disabled and suffered over 60 casualties as she fell back on Hood. Then it was the Germans' turn to suffer: *Invincible*, *Inflexible* and *Indomitable* came into action at about 8,000 yards (7,280 m) and the thin-skinned cruisers were engulfed by giant shell splashes. *Pillau* had her bridge wrecked, four boilers knocked out and her speed reduced. *Wiesbaden* was targeted by *Invincible*, whose gunnery was superb on this, her last day afloat. A 12-in. (305 mm) shell burst in her engine room, leaving *Wiesbaden* dead in the water.

The destroyers *Shark*, *Ophelia*, *Acasta* and *Christopher* put on speed to deliver a torpedo attack. Unfortunately, Hipper's flotilla commander gave the same order: the four British destroyers met a dozen German torpedo boats in a whirling fight. The cruiser *Regensburg* disabled the *Shark* which also took a torpedo under her stern from *G 41*. The German flotillas found the battle cruisers were visible only when illuminated by the flash from their broadsides. Hood ordered evasive action and his

ships 'combed' the torpedo tracks, although *Invincible* momentarily came to a complete stop when her helm jammed. Midshipman Frank Layard, in the foretop of *Indomitable,* saw 'a torpedo, with its red warhead and propellers slowly revolving, passing slowly down our port side on the surface not ten yards from us.'[15]

Shark foundered, having fired her torpedoes. Her commander, Loftus-Jones won a posthumous VC for continuing the fight despite mortal injuries to his ship and himself.

The crippled *Wiesbaden* attracted new predators, the 3rd and 4th Light Cruiser Squadrons of the Grand Fleet. Konteradmiral Behncke turned III Geschwader two points and put on speed, all four Königs blasting away with their secondary armament, but the British cruisers continued to attack. Hipper steered for the *Wiesbaden,* but was attacked by the destroyers *Onslow* and *Acasta*. *Acasta* was badly hit by Hipper's flagship and made off, enveloped in smoke. *Onslow* was also hit by *Lützow,* but torpedoed *Wiesbaden* from point blank range, then braved a storm of shot to launch a solo attack on III Geschwader. *Kaiser* had to alter course to avoid one torpedo but no hits were scored. *Onslow* should have been destroyed, but her captain, Lieutenant-Commander Tovey, lived to fight another day—and sink the *Bismarck* in 1941.

Onslow made her escape as the German Dreadnoughts shifted fire to larger targets. The *Wiesbaden* had been spotted by the fire-eating Admiral Arbuthnot who led *Defence, Warrior* and *Black Prince* into the fray – without regard for any other squadron, British or German. Armoured cruisers had been made redundant by the advent of the battle cruiser: that was the lesson from the battles of the Falklands and Dogger Bank. But Arbuthnot's squadron thrust into action regardless; Beatty's battle cruisers were forced to alter course to avoid a collision. *Defence* opened fire at 1805hrs but within ten minutes she was spotted by Hipper's battle cruisers and the leading German Dreadnoughts. The range was less than 8,000 yards (7,280 m), *Derfflinger* even launched a torpedo.

Defence took a hit on her after 9.2-in. (234 mm) turret which exploded its magazine. Her side turrets erupted, one-by-one, in a series of sympathetic detonations until her forward magazine went too and she vanished in a thunderclap heard by both fleets. There were no survivors.

1730: The light cruiser *Chester* scouts ahead of Hood's 3rd Battle Squadron, and encounters the German light cruiser screen of II Aufklärungsgruppe, *Frankfurt, Pillau, Elbing,* and *Wiesbaden. Chester* is disabled and loses 60 men.

Hood's 3rd Battle Cruiser Squadron led by *Invincible.* intervention of the 3rd BCS prevented the German cru observing the deployment of the Grand Fleet and *Invinc* inflicted mortal damage on the *Lützow* be her own destruc

Armoured cruiser *Cochrane.*

1720HRS: The Grand Fleet steaming in six columns each of four Dreadnoughts at full speed, 23-24 knots. The 4th Light Cruiser Squadron was accompanied by the armoured cruisers *Hampshire, Minotaur* and *Shannon.*

LIGHT WIND

Ist Cruiser Squadron, led by *Black Prince* at the starboard end of the armoured cruiser screen steaming ahead of the Grand Fleet. With *Duke of Edinburgh* and *Warrior*, Admiral Arbuthnot aboard *Defence* led his squadron to destruction by charging the *Wiesbaden* and running into the German battle cruisers.

THE RUN TO THE NORTH 1710 – 1735HRS

Now it was the turn of the British to lure the enemy on to a larger opponent, and they steered for the estimated position of the Grand Fleet. Another series of signalling errors exposed Britain's four most powerful battleships to the van of the German fleet, and they engaged the eight leading German battleships for nearly half an hour. Any loss of speed would have entailed their destruction.

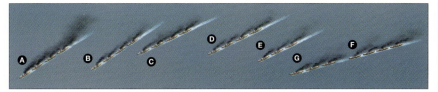

A: *König* (Konteradmiral Behncke), *Grosser Kurfürst, Markgraf, Kronprinz*; B: *Kaiser* (Konteradmiral Nordmann), *Prinzregent Luitpold, Kaiserin*; C: *Friedrich der Große,* (Vizeadmiral Scheer) *Ostfriesland* (Vizeadmiral Schmidt), *Thüringen, Helgoland, Oldenburg*; D: *Posen* (Konteradmiral Engelhardt), *Rheinland, Nassau, Westfalen*; E: *Deutschland* (Konteradmiral Mauve), *Pommern, Schliesen*; F: *Hannover* (Konteradmiral Von Dalwigk zu Lichtenfels), *Schleswig-Holstein, Hessen*; G: **IV Aufklärungsgruppe** - *Stettin* (KzS von Reuter), *München, Frauenlob, Stuttgart, Hamburg.*

Following the order 'GENERAL CHASE', the König class battleships *Lützow, Derfflinger, Seydlitz, Moltke* and *Von der Tann* are exceeding their designed speed in their attempts to catch the British.

5th Battle Squadron (led by *Barham*) with 2nd Light Cruiser Squadron about to pass to the disengaged side, both under heavy fire from the German van. The 5th BS does not return fire, but steers into the shell splashes to avoid the German salvoes.

The seaplane carrier *Engadine* sent up a reconnaissance plane at 1530hrs, but overall visibility was poor. By 1700hrs conditions are deteriorating steadily, with smog from the gunfire and engine smoke contributing to the misty weather.

The 1st and 3rd Light Cruiser Squadrons and Beatty's First Battle Cruisers (*Lion, Princess Royal, Tiger* and *New Zealand*).

The magnificent lines of *Tiger*, the most modern of the British battle cruisers at Jutland. Influenced by the *Kongo*, built by Vickers for Japan, she survived 15 hits by 11-in. (279 mm) shells during the battle. Her fighting ability was not seriously reduced: a classic illustration of the role of chance in naval warfare. (IWM)

Warrior was shattered and ablaze, but managed to limp away just as the 5th Battle Squadron re-entered the fray. *Black Prince* escaped without serious damage.

During Arbuthnot's meteoric intervention Evan-Thomas endeavoured to follow Beatty, who was steaming hard to take station ahead of the Grand Fleet. But the Dreadnoughts were turning into line of battle and he would have had to pass dangerously close, masking their guns. Instead, he followed *Marlborough*'s division at the rear of the line where his squadron was abeam of Scheer's centre. Unfortunately visibility improved here to give the German battleships the first clear target they had seen. Scheer's flagship, *Friedrich der Große*, fired its first broadside at 1820hrs, at least four other battleships engaging the 5th BS with both main and secondary armaments at 10–15,000 yards (9,100–13,650 m). Their fury lasted about 20 minutes before *Ostfriesland* checked fire, their targets no longer visible in the failing light. *Warspite*'s steering failed and she suffered 13 hits by heavy shells while circling twice, inadvertently saving the *Warrior*.

By 1830hrs the battleships of the Grand Fleet formed a single line, bent at either end, with a few ships overlapping. The rearmost squadron was on a north-easterly course, turning to follow the main body east-south-east. The foremost division, led by *King George V*, was turning east to avoid the battle cruisers as they cut in front.

Lion, *Princess Royal*, *Tiger* and the *New Zealand* passed the fleet and turned south-east astern of Hood's squadron, with the 3rd Light Cruiser Squadron in between. They spotted the German battle cruisers straggling eastwards about 5 miles (8 km) to the south. Directly behind them came the High Sea Fleet in line ahead, the gun battle between the centre of Scheer's line and the British 5th BS visible only as momentary stabs of orange in the twilight. The noise, however, was unmistakable.

The battle cruiser fleets had a furious exchange of fire, with hideous consequences for another of Beatty's big ships and the first major German casualty. But as they resumed their fight, the leading German battleships became visible from *King George V* and the 2nd Battle Squadron. Most of the 4th Battle Squadron saw them too, as did the *Iron Duke* and several of the rearmost battleships. *König* drew the heaviest fire, with both 15-in. (381 mm)-gunned 'super Dreadnoughts', *Revenge* and *Royal Oak*, opening fire on her, as well as five or six 13.5-in. (343 mm) gun battleships including the British flagship. *Iron Duke*'s

gunnery was fast – nine salvoes in five minutes – and she hit hard. At the rear of the British line an apparent explosion marked the awe-inspiring debut of the *Agincourt* with her 14 12-in. (305 mm) guns firing a full salvo – 'like a Brocks' benefit' according to an observer on *Malaya*.

Few battleships saw more than a limited part of the enemy battle line in the gathering gloom. Only a handful of the German battleships could make out a clear target. *Prinzregent Luitpold* opened fire on *King George V*. *König* reeled under the repeated impact of heavy shells. Standing on the upper bridge, Konteradmiral Behncke was wounded when a shell ricocheted from the roof of the armoured conning tower below. In minutes she was on fire, her decks choked with gas from the explosions, and listing perceptibly. As Scheer described it, 'The entire arc stretching from north to east was a sea of fire. The flash from the muzzles of the guns was distinctly seen through the mist and smoke though the ships themselves were not distinguishable.'[16]

Hipper's flagship suffered a succession of hits. Already shipping a considerable quantity of water forward, *Lützow* sustained two 12-in. (305 mm) hits from *Invincible* that caused severe flooding. *Moltke* thought the squadron was under fire from about ten battleships. *Derfflinger* was zig-zagging rather than maintain her position in the line under the fire of the British battle cruisers. Admiral Hood could see his flagship's shells straddling the *Lützow* and told his gunnery officer, Lieutenant-Commander Dannreuther, to 'keep it up, every shot is telling'. Dannreuther had just finished passing on the admiral's

Jellicoe's flagship *Iron Duke* fired nine salvoes in five minutes when the König class battleships loomed out of the murk at about 1830hrs. *König* was hit hard, coming under fire from two 15-in. (381 mm) gun Revenge class battleships as well. (IWM)

OVERLEAF **Fleet action, 1830hrs. The view from *Iron Duke* - the magnificent sight of Dreadnoughts in line astern. *Royal Oak* fires on the German battle cruisers. In the distance, *Wiesbaden* is on fire, although one gun is still in action.**

LEFT **1833hrs: Admiral Hood tells his gunnery officer in the foretop, 'keep it up, every shot is telling' as the *Invincible* hits the *Lützow* and *Derfflinger* with successive salvoes. Then a salvo from *Derfflinger* strikes with the terrible effect seen here. *Invincible* blew up seconds later as her magazines detonated and Hood and 1,020 officers and men were killed. Her gunnery officer and several other men in the foretop found themselves in the water, but alive. (IWM)**

Kaiser was narrowly missed by a torpedo and hit repeatedly during Scheer's second accidental head-on encounter with the British battle line. During the twilight phase she engaged British destroyers and light cruisers, driving off elements of the 4th Destroyer Flotilla. After the battle, it fell to her to drop a buoy to mark the mines left by the *Abdiel*, later mistaken for a submarine periscope by some of the German pre-Dreadnoughts. (IWM)

compliments to the turret commanders when, 5 miles (8 km) south, 'the veil of mist in front of us split across like the curtain at the theatre' as Von Hase remembered. *Invincible* was 'steering an almost parallel course with ours, at top speed. Her guns were trained on us and immediately another salvo crashed out, straddling us completely.'[17] *Derfflinger* fired back, hits were observed amidships and *Invincible* was ripped apart by a savage succession of explosions. She broke in half, her bow and stern sections projecting from the shallow seabed.

The German battle cruisers turned away due south. The *König* followed, but to turn the German battle line in succession would have been suicidal. Scheer ordered a *Gefechtskehrtwendung* (battle about-turn). It was supposed to be started by the rearmost ship, the next ahead putting over her helm once the vessel astern had begun her turn, and it should have been initiated by the pre-Dreadnoughts. They lagged behind, so KzS Redlich, commanding the rearmost Dreadnought, *Westfalen*, commenced the turn on his own initiative. As events that night were to prove, he was a highly capable officer commanding a crew that really knew its business.

German torpedo boats sped to the head of the line as the turn began and laid a smokescreen. As they retired from this mission, Kommodore Michelson (*Rostock*) encountered the *Lützow*, under ferocious fire from the British battle cruisers. The *G 39* went alongside to take off Hipper and his staff; four other boats laid smoke and Hipper's squadron escaped to the west.

The destroyer *Badger* received an order from *Lion* to 'PICK UP SURVIVORS FROM WRECK STARBOARD SIDE'. They saw the bows and stern of what they thought was a German light cruiser projecting from the water. As *Badger* picked her way through the flotsam of kitbags, hammocks and decking, four men were seen on a raft and two more in the water. The destroyer's whaler was sent away in charge of a gunner, flourishing his revolver. Armed marines and the doctor waited on the deck. To their surprise, aboard the raft they found Lieutenant-Commander Dannreuther and only five other survivors from the *Invincible*. Admiral Hood and 1,020 officers and men lay entombed in the wreck.

The Germans had been drifting in and out of sight from the moment they were seen, and it was not obvious to Jellicoe that they had broken off the action. *Iron Duke* checked fire at 1836hrs, most British battleships losing their targets at about the same time. At 1844hrs Jellicoe altered course by divisions, steering south-east, then to due south at 1855hrs. He never thought of following Scheer into the murk where German torpedo boats could ambush his line from close range. Instead, he placed his fleet across the German line of retreat.

Marlborough was torpedoed at this time and reduced to 17 knots, although she kept her place in the line. It is not known who fired at her: at the time it was thought to be the parting shot of the *Wiesbaden*, barely afloat but only 9,000 yards (8,190 m) from the British, although another cripple, *V 48* (sunk by gunfire by elements of the British 4th Destroyer Flotilla), may have been responsible. *Marlborough* opened fire with her main armament, sending two of the *Wiesbaden*'s funnels overboard and setting her ablaze from stem to stern. The battleship hit her with a torpedo for good measure, but the cruiser still refused to sink.

No one on *Neptune*'s bridge spotted a torpedo coming at them: fortunately a gunnery lieutenant did, and bellowed 'hard-a-starboard' into the helmsman's voice-pipe. The captain ordered emergency full speed. An officer in the foretop was one of the survivors of the pre-Dreadnought *Formidable*, torpedoed in 1915 with the loss of over 500 men. He craned his neck over the side as the top vibrated with the strain of the great ship turning at emergency speed with full helm on. 'The torpedo was now dead astern following our exact course, but going faster than our fastest speed, and coming closer and closer until our view from the fore-top was blanketed by the main mast.' They waited in grim silence, but there was no explosion. Either the torpedo was deflected by the battleship's wash or ran its range out.

By 1900hrs the Grand Fleet was steering south by divisions: six columns each of four battleships echeloned so that the most easterly division (led by *King George V*) was about 2 miles (3 km) farther south than the most westerly (led by *Marlborough*). Evan-Thomas followed *Marlborough*'s division. The battle cruisers were 5,000 yards (4,550 m) south-east of *King George V*, steaming on the same course, with *Inflexible* and *Indomitable* astern of *New Zealand*. Beatty slowed down to remain in

The second class of German Dreadnoughts, the Helgolands carried a high velocity 12-in. (305 mm) gun to counter the 13.5-in. (343 mm) guns of their British equivalents, the Orion class. However, they retained the inefficient hexagonal turret layout of the earlier Nassau class. *Helgoland*, seen here, was hit by a 15-in. (381 mm) shell at Jutland which caused considerable damage. (IWM)

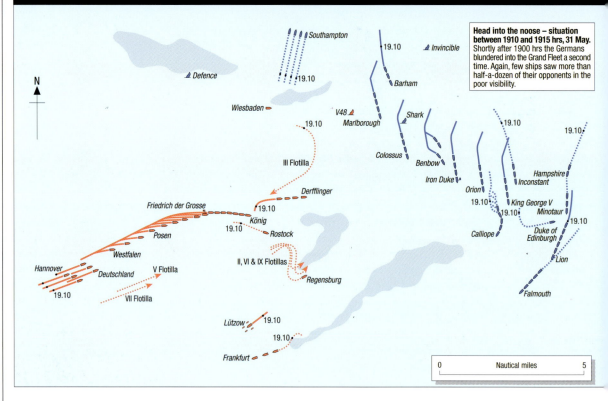

Head into the noose – situation between 1910 and 1915 hrs, 31 May. Shortly after 1900 hrs the Germans blundered into the Grand Fleet a second time. Again, few ships saw more than half-a-dozen of their opponents in the poor visibility.

close contact with the battle fleet and a gyro failure sent *Lion* in a complete circle before control was re-established.

There was an hour's daylight remaining, two at the most. But where were the Germans? Incredibly, they had reversed course by means of a second *Gefechtskehrtwendung*. Battle cruisers in the van, Scheer's fleet was 7 miles (11 km) south-east of the most westerly division of the Grand Fleet. The Germans headed east in a premature attempt to break past the British. Scheer's mendacious account of the battle represents this as a spoiling attack, and is supported by the German *Official History*, but if Scheer's intention was to disrupt the enemy at twilight, a properly conducted attack by his flotillas would have served. Instead, the German line steered directly at the British. Scheer put his neck back into the noose.

Shortly after 1900hrs Jellicoe saw that his starboard divisions were in action again. He could not see their targets: the Königs, Hipper's battle cruisers and several torpedo boats attempting to reach the *Wiesbaden*. The latter came under such fierce fire from the British battleships that they put about, firing torpedoes that passed between the Dreadnoughts. Then Jellicoe observed the unmistakable silhouettes of the German battle fleet emerge some 10,000 yards (9,100 m) from his flagship.

For a few desperate minutes after 1910hrs Scheer's line was subjected to intense fire against which little reply was possible. The Königs took the brunt, *König* was hit once (by *Iron Duke*), *Grosser Kurfürst* was hit four times and even *Helgoland*, four ships astern of Scheer's flagship, took a 15-in. (381 mm) shell near the waterline forward. The British ships were invisible to the Germans. The horizon appeared to be on fire, rippling orange flashes in a broad arc across their line of advance. Scheer ordered a third *Gefechtskehrtwendung*. His desperation can be gauged by the signals he sent to the battle cruisers at 1913hrs: by flag, 'Battle cruisers at the Enemy! Give it everything!', and by radio, 'Battle cruisers turn toward the enemy and engage him closely! At him!'

All the German battle cruisers were seriously damaged apart from the *Moltke*. Nevertheless, they obeyed Scheer's desperate order and steamed at full speed into the guns of the Grand Fleet.

KzS von Egidy took in Scheer's signal and ordered the ratings manning the telephones in the conning tower to pass it to the crew. 'From Captain to Ship: Signal from C-in-C Fleet: *Schlachtkreuzer ran*!' Stations throughout the *Seydlitz* reported they had received the message and 'there followed a kind of awed hush for a moment, the ship seemed to hold its breath'. Then, through the voice pipes, the ventilation shafts and the armoured passageways, came the sound of cheering, and the stirring strains of *Wacht am Rhein*. In the fiery light below, the stokers hammered their shovels against the bulkheads, shouting 'Drauf *Seydlitz*' [Attack *Seydlitz*!], the war cry of the Seydlitz cuirassiers of Frederick the Great's army.

Derfflinger's 'C' turret was penetrated by a 15-in. (381 mm) shell, the explosion ignited the propellent charges and burned to death 73 of the 78 men in the turret. Then another 15-in. (381 mm) shell smashed the

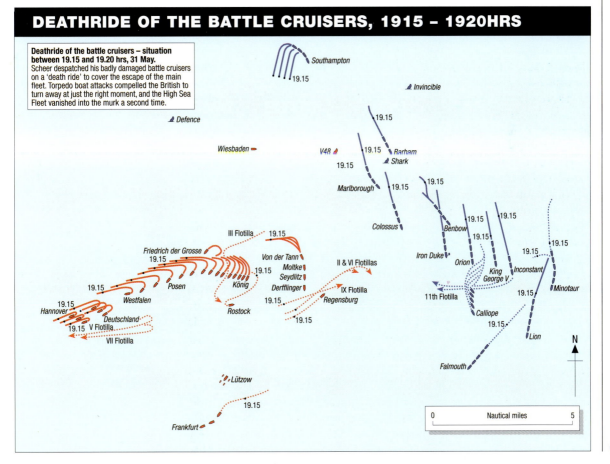

DEATHRIDE OF THE BATTLE CRUISERS, 1915 – 1920HRS

Deathride of the battle cruisers – situation between 19.15 and 19.20 hrs, 31 May.
Scheer despatched his badly damaged battle cruisers on a 'death ride' to cover the escape of the main fleet. Torpedo boat attacks compelled the British to turn away at just the right moment, and the High Sea Fleet vanished into the murk a second time.

roof of 'D' turret with similar, ghastly consequences – one man was blown clear but the other 80 men inside were killed. The ship filled with poisonous gases from the explosions and von Hase gave the order to don gas masks. The *Von der Tann* was hit too, power failure plunging her below-decks compartments into darkness.

By 1915hrs this maritime Balaklava brought the battle cruisers to within four miles of the nearest British Dreadnoughts when KzS Hartog made out a flag signal flying on the *Friedrich der Große* ordering them to engage the head of the enemy line. They turned on to a parallel course with the British, covering the retirement of Scheer's main body. At 1920hrs the battle cruisers bore away to the west, their escape coinciding with a mass attack by German torpedo boats.

The battle fleet's about-turn was chaotic, but Scheer's captains managed it without a collision. Scheer took his flagship to port, rather than to starboard as he ordered the rest of the fleet, as the battleships were dangerously bunched and some were squeezed out of the line. *König* laid a smokescreen, as did *Kaiser*, although she was hit repeatedly even after she turned.

Scheer ordered his flotillas to attack and generate a smokescreen. Six flotillas, carrying a total of 224 torpedoes, were available. The attack was led by VI and IX Torpedobootsflotillen, which raced towards the British, leaving a thick trail of smoke in their wake. They attacked from about 8,000 yards (7,280 m). Five boats of III Torpedobootsflotille attacked next, but those of VII Torpedobootsflotille could not reach an attack position and remained off the port bow of II Geschwader. Jellicoe's reaction was to turn away, by two points at 1922hrs and another two at 1925hrs until the fleet split into sub-divisions steering south-east. *Marlborough*, *Colossus*, *Hercules* and *Agincourt* all had to turn hard to avoid torpedoes; one passed between *Iron Duke* and *Thunderer*; *Revenge* had to put her helm over twice in succession as two pairs of torpedoes sped past. The British fired with both main and secondary armaments, *Iron Duke* sinking the *S 35* with two hits from her 13.5-in. (343 mm) guns.

By turning away, Jellicoe avoided any casualties but passed up the opportunity to crush the High Sea Fleet. The German battleships were in disarray, unable to co-ordinate their gunnery. But the British did not know the extent of the Germans' difficulties. Scheer's turn was not observed; Jellicoe assumed his opponent had made an eight-point turn to widen the range, and so ordered his own fleet to proceed south-by-west, still steaming in sub-divisions. Scheer reorganised his squadrons, steering due south with the battle cruisers on his port beam.

In ships of both fleets, damage control parties hurried to restore power, get guns back into action, extinguish fires and deal with the wounded. Unless a ship had suffered catastrophic punishment, few people aboard were aware of anything but their immediate surroundings. The big ships' turrets had crews of up to 70 men. There were large teams between decks – supplying ammunition to the secondary batteries, the fire and repair parties, and the entire engineering complement – none had much indication of the progress of the battle. There were clues, violent changes of course and speed, the secondary guns going to rapid fire, the jarring vibration of the hull after a heavy shell hit home, but most men at Jutland knew little of what occurred on their own ship and next to nothing of the wider picture. A midshipman in *Malaya*'s torpedo control tower remembers one terrifying moment: 'there came a sudden shudder and lurch through the ship, a frightful din of escaping steam, and the ship took on an uncomfortable list to starboard'.[18] It was followed by 'tender enquiries' from the torpedo flats, switch-board and other stations below decks. The same observer used the lull after 1930hrs to inspect the 6-in. (152 mm) battery 'where everything was dark chaos. Most of the wounded had been taken away, but several of the killed were still there. The most ghastly part of the whole affair was the smell of burnt human flesh, which remained in the ship for weeks.'

In engine rooms, the back-breaking effort required to maintain full steam took its toll. 'Anyone brought up in the oil-fuel age can have no idea of the physical effort required of the stokers of a coal-fired ship steaming at high speed. With the fans supplying air to the boilers whirring at full speed the furnaces devoured coal just about as fast as a man could feed them. Black, begrimed and sweating men working in the bunkers in the ship's side dug the coal out and loaded it into skids which were then dragged along the steel deck and emptied on to the floorplates in front of each boiler...Looking down from the iron catwalk above, the scene had all the appearance of one from Dante's Inferno.'[19]

Warrior was ablaze along the mess deck. The heart of the fire lay in the gunnery office, around a corner where no hose could reach it. Paint

Acasta (4th Destroyer Flotilla) carried out a torpedo attack on Hipper's flagship *Lützow* but was crippled by gunfire and lucky to escape. Sisterships *Ardent*, *Sparrowhawk* and *Shark* were sunk at Jutland. Displacing 1,072 tons, the 20-strong Acasta class were armed with two 21-in. (533 mm) torpedo tubes, with four torpedoes, and 3 x 4-in. (102 mm) guns. (IWM)

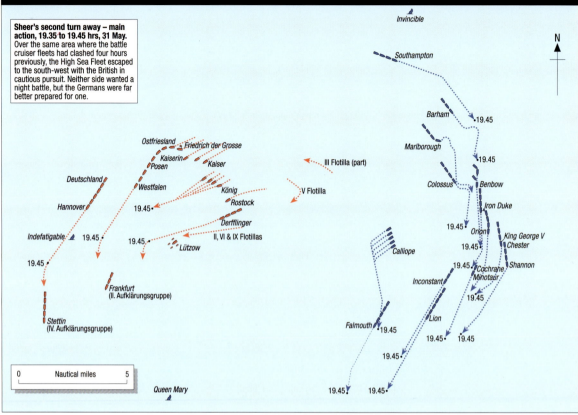

SCHEER'S SECOND TURN-AWAY - MAIN ACTION 1935–1945HRS

Scheer's second turn away – main action, 19.35 to 19.45 hrs, 31 May. Over the same area where the battle cruiser fleets had clashed four hours previously, the High Sea Fleet escaped to the south-west with the British in cautious pursuit. Neither side wanted a night battle, but the Germans were far better prepared for one.

blistered, corticene decking melted to a black, resinous, ooze. The heat was too intense for anyone to enter the compartment. It took two hours to beat back the flames which were eventually extinguished by a man climbing down the ship's side and playing the hose through the entry hole made by the shell. The engine rooms were flooded, the fire trapping the survivors at the top of the compartment, where they had to endure blasts of scalding steam while up to their necks in water, hanging on to the upper gratings. If they let go, they were sucked under and into the racing cranks below – the engines kept working until water was halfway up the cylinders. They splashed the oily water over their faces to protect them from the steam, and clung on, in pitch darkness, not even knowing if the ship had been abandoned until someone heard the click of a valve being operated somewhere above. There were eight men at the grating when the water stopped rising. Only three were still alive two and a half hours later, when the fire above them was put out, the armoured hatch lifted and the rescue party heard the men shouting.

Parting shots

The British 4th LCS and 11th DF ran into boats of V Torpedobootsflotille and chased the torpedo boats astern of the German battle cruisers until they encountered the centre of Scheer's line. A brief exchange of fire followed, *Prinzregent Luitpold*, *Markgraf* and *Kaiser* all engaging with main and secondary armament. The British turned away, only the cruiser

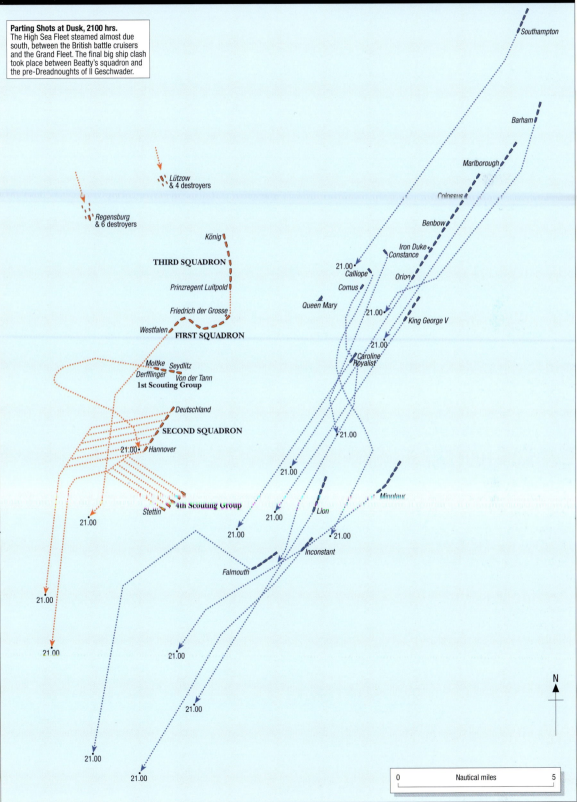

Parting Shots at Dusk, 2100 hrs.
The High Sea Fleet steamed almost due south, between the British battle cruisers and the Grand Fleet. The final big ship clash took place between Beatty's squadron and the pre-Dreadnoughts of II Geschwader.

Southampton

Barham

Marlborough

Colossus

Benbow

Lützow
& 4 destroyers

Regensburg
& 6 destroyers

König

Iron Duke
Constance

THIRD SQUADRON

21.00
Calliope

Orion

Prinzregent Luitpold

Comus

Friedrich der Grosse

Queen Mary

21.00

Westfalen

FIRST SQUADRON

King George V

21.00

Moltke   Seydlitz
Derfflinger   Von der Tann
1st Scouting Group

Caroline
Royalist

Deutschland

SECOND SQUADRON

21.00

21.00 • Hannover

4th Scouting Group

Minotaur

Stettin

21.00

Lion

21.00

21.00

Inconstant

21.00

Falmouth

21.00

21.00

21.00

N

0   Nautical miles   5

21.00

21.00

69

Calliope ventured to launch a torpedo. It missed and she suffered
33 casualties before getting clear.

Meanwhile, cruisers at the head of both fleets fought a spirited action
just after 2000hrs. Rear-Admiral Napier's 3rd LCS (*Falmouth, Yarmouth,
Birkenhead* and *Gloucester*) plus *Canterbury* encountered Kommodore von
Reuter's IV Aufklärungsgruppe (*Stettin, Munchen, Frauenlob, Stuttgart* and
Hamburg). Silhouetted against the lighter western horizon, the Germans
could see little of their opponents other than gunflashes; after sustaining
several hits, von Reuter's squadron turned away due west.

The cruiser action was heard from the bridge of *Lion* and gunflashes
seen in the distance. Beatty turned to investigate and was rewarded at
2018hrs by the sight of his old enemies, the German battle cruisers, on his
starboard beam at about 8,500 yards (7,735 m). They caught Hipper in the
act of transferring from *G 39* to the *Moltke*. Again, the Germans could
barely make out their assailants and although they managed to score a hit
on *Princess Royal* and another on *Lion*, *Seydlitz* and *Derfflinger* were hit
twice, and the latter left without any functioning main armament. Hipper
made off to the west, and was finally able to board *Moltke* at 2115hrs. His
escape was covered by the 'five-minute ships', the pre-Dreadnoughts of

The Orion class were part of the 1909 naval programme that included eight Dreadnoughts. Scare-mongering and political lobbying had doubled the number of new battleships ('We Want Eight and We Won't Wait' was the slogan) in the wake of the Austrian annexation of Bosnia-Herzegovina. Armed with 10 x 13.5-in. (343 mm) guns, the Orions were completed in 1912 and all four fought at Jutland. (Author's Collection)

II Geschwader which turned south-west to bring their full broadsides to bear. In the gloom, *Schleswig-Holstein* and *Pommern* could not see a target, but *Deutschland, Hannover, Schlesien* and *Hessen* did, although their shots went wide. British retaliation was swift, three of the pre-Dreadnoughts were hit, *Pommern* hauling out of the line for a few minutes. Konteradmiral Mauve ordered an eight-point turn to starboard at 2035hrs and was relieved to find the British did not follow. Beatty pressed on south-west, oblivious that he had steamed across the path of the High Sea Fleet. By 2100hrs he was steering south-south-east with the German battle fleet following, out of sight, 10 miles (16 km) astern.

Cruisers ahead of the Grand Fleet caught a glimpse of the German battleships, but the enemy was where they expected to see Beatty's battle cruisers. Admiral Jerram stopped *Caroline* and *Royalist* from making a torpedo attack, fearing a 'blue-on-blue', and radioed Jellicoe that he could see the British 1st BCS. It was actually I Geschwader. *Westfalen* and *Nassau* gave the game away at 2108hrs, firing on the 11th DF at 8,000 yards (7,280m) before turning six points to port – they assumed the British were about to launch torpedoes. But the Germans vanished as suddenly as they had appeared; the sun had set more than half-an-hour previously and there were but a few minutes of dim light before darkness shrouded the sea.

Beatty reported to Jellicoe at 2059hrs, identifying enemy battleships and pre-Dreadnoughts at 10–11 miles (16–18 km), steering south-west. The Grand Fleet and High Sea Fleet were now on gently converging courses, but neither side wanted a night action: both feared catastrophic losses from torpedoes.

In the nightmare of the dark

Scheer ordered his fleet to steer for the Horns Reef. The *Lützow* was left behind to make her own way to safety if she could. II Geschwader was ordered back from the van, taking station astern of the two Dreadnought squadrons. *Westfalen* led the battle fleet home. The battle cruisers split up: *Derfflinger* and *Von der Tann*, both practically disarmed, followed the pre-Dreadnoughts. *Lützow* lagged 10 miles (16 km) astern, almost awash, her bulkheads severely stressed. *Moltke* and *Seydlitz* found themselves ahead of the battle line, some way to port.

There were three routes open to Scheer. He could head north and into the Kattegat – but this would leave him at sea throughout 1 June, exposed to being overhauled by the faster British fleet. He could make for the Dutch coast and cut behind the minefields in the Heligoland Bight to reach the Ems estuary. The third, shortest, route was to steer south-east for the Horns Reef and down the swept channel outside the Amrum Bank.

Jellicoe covered both options, proceeding towards the Bight where he could intercept the Germans if they made for the southerly escape route to the Ems. To reach the Horns Reef, Scheer would have to pass astern of the Grand Fleet where Jellicoe massed his destroyers. For added insurance, he despatched the fast minelayer *Abdiel* to lay mines off the Horns Reef. Three British submarines (*E 55, E 26* and *D 1*) lay off the Vyl lightship.

Hampshire, and to the south, *Minotaur, Shannon* and *Cochrane*.

Invincible lies broken in half, her bows and stern projecting from the water after her magazines exploded.

The Grand Fleet Dreadnoughts deploy into line of battle, the 5th Battle Squadron taking station astern. Fire is concentrated on the German van and on the crippled *Wiesbaden*.

2nd and 1st Light Cruiser Squadrons.

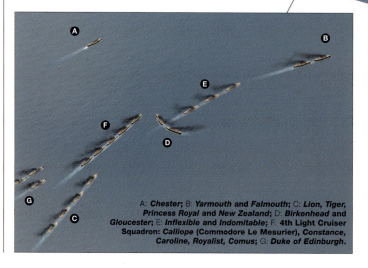

A: *Chester*; B: *Yarmouth* and *Falmouth*; C: *Lion, Tiger, Princess Royal* and *New Zealand*; D: *Birkenhead* and *Gloucester*; E: *Inflexible* and *Indomitable*; F: 4th Light Cruiser Squadron: *Calliope* (Commodore Le Mesurier), *Constance, Caroline, Royalist, Comus*; G: *Duke of Edinburgh*.

König, Grosser Kurfürst, Markgraf , and *Kronprinz* sustain heavy damage as they are subject to concentrated fire.

Crippled armoured cruiser *Warrior* shelters in the lee of *Warspite* as she circles out of control.

Wiesbaden was left dead in the water after *Invincible* put a 12-in. shell in her boiler room. Lying in the path of the Grand Fleet, she came under fire from a succession of British battleships, but kept at least one gun in action until the end. The devotion of her crew was praised by Admiral Jellicoe.

Shark sinking: her commander, Loftus-Jones would be awarded a posthumous VC for pressing home his torpedo attack despite his own mortal injuries.

Light cruiser *Rostock* leads III Flotille in a torpedo attack.

THE MAIN ACTION 1826 – 1835HRS

Jellicoe successfully deployed the Grand Fleet to cross the German 'T', subjecting the German line to the might of the British Dreadnoughts.

Hipper's battle cruisers are driven back by the weight of fire, his flagship *Lützow* shipping thousands of tons of water and in danger of foundering.

Regensburg with II, VI and IX Flotille. II Aufklärungsgruppe (Konteradmiral Bödicker) *Frankfurt, Pillau, Elbing*.

V Flotille and VII Flotille

Posen, Rheinland, Nassau, Westfalen.

The pre-Dreadnoughts have fallen behind after Scheer ordered 'GENERAL CHASE' and the leading dreadnoughts put on full steam to keep up with the 5th Battle Squadron.

Kaiser, Prinzregent Luitpold, Kaiserin.

From his flagship, *Friedrich der Große*, Scheer is confronted by 'a sea of fire': he has blundered headfirst into the Grand Fleet.

LIGHT WIND

Hercules fires at night. The High Sea Fleet was far better prepared for night fighting than the British, but its training was primarily defensive: Scheer was no more keen on a nocturnal mêlée than Jellicoe. (IWM)

Light cruisers *Frankfurt* and *Pillau* steamed up the port side of the High Sea Fleet. IV Aufklärungsgruppe was supposed to be covering the starboard side, but Kommodore von Reuter was actually on the port side, followed by the damaged *Elbing* and *Rostock*. The error was fortuitous: it placed a powerful formation of light cruisers between the High Sea Fleet and the British light forces that might otherwise have located the German main body. *Hamburg* and *Elbing* had a brief exchange of shots with elements of the British 11th Destroyer Flotilla led by *Castor*. The Germans used the British recognition signal then fired at little more than 1,000 yards (910 m). Both sides launched torpedoes, *Castor* and *Hamburg* were struck by several shells then both veered away into the night.

Von Reuter's squadron had barely re-formed when the giant silhouettes of *Moltke* and *Seydlitz* loomed out of the darkness, forcing *Stettin* to slow down and her consorts to turn to port. *München*, *Frauenlob* and *Stuttgart* sighted more ships a few hundred yards away. They flashed the German recognition signal and received a hail of fire from the 2nd Light Cruiser Squadron. *Southampton* and *Dublin* switched on their searchlights and became targets for the whole German squadron, but *Nottingham* and *Birmingham* were only visible as gunflashes. Von Reuter turned away, all his ships hit. *Frauenlob* capsized, hit by a torpedo from *Southampton*. The British sheered off too, both leading cruisers on fire.

Moltke and *Seydlitz* became separated. *Moltke* subsequently had three close encounters with British battleship squadrons, but each time managed to slip back into the night. She was seen from *Thunderer*, but Captain Ferguson thought it better not to shoot — that, he thought, would betray the position of the battle fleet. At least *Moltke* could defend herself: *Seydlitz* could neither fight nor run away. She too had the eerie experience of sighting the solid outlines of capital ships, her people wondering if this was the prelude to a final crashing series of broadsides. *Agincourt* saw her, but her captain was of the same mould as Ferguson. *Revenge* had a glimpse, but her giant 15-in. (381 mm) guns stayed silent.

The Nassau class, Germany's first Dreadnoughts, combined an inefficient turret layout with reciprocating machinery that limited them to less than 20 knots. The wing turrets enabled six guns to bear fore and aft, but their weight compelled the designers to place the secondary armament in casemates unworkable in a seaway. *Nassau* collided with the *Spitfire* during the night, leaving a section of her plating on the destroyer. (IWM)

Agincourt leads the 4th Battle Squadron in 1915. Part of the 1st Battle Squadron at Jutland, she fired on the High Sea Fleet during the tantalisingly short gunnery duel. Her officers spotted the *Seydlitz* during the night, but her captain refused to open fire without orders and von Egidy's crippled battle cruiser was allowed to escape. (IWM)

OVERLEAF **Deathride of the German battle cruisers, 1910hrs. Scheer's line steered directly at the British ships, attempting to break past them, but they were engaged by Jellicoe's Dreadnoughts and suffered terrible damage. Scheer ordered *Gefechtskehrtwendung*, the battle about turn, which was chaotic, but achieved without collision. In the foreground, *Derfflinger* is turning at speed, with both 'C' and 'D' turrets damaged. *Seydlitz* is low in the water behind her, the waves breaking over her bows.**

Only after the battle did the gunnery officer of *Marlborough* lament that he should have disobeyed his captain's orders not to fire on the strange ship he observed at only 4,000 yards (3,640 m). The Nordic gods guarding *Seydlitz* saw her through the 2-mile (3.2 km) gap between the British 2nd and 5th Battle Squadrons, and she wallowed home unharmed. Her engines were giving revolutions for 20 knots, but she was so heavily flooded that her actual speed was anyone's guess, her navigation uncertain too. Hand soundings were made and she went aground twice before passing the Horns Reef lightship at 0400hrs.

By 2300hrs the German battle fleet was approaching the British 5th Battle Squadron, bearing roughly 140 degrees from the *Barham*. In between, in a line about three miles long, was the 4th Destroyer Flotilla led by Captain Wintour in the *Tipperary*. Wintour suddenly realised there was a line of battleships dangerously close on his starboard quarter, the leading one little more than 1,000 yards away and closing. He flashed the recognition signal and was immediately illuminated by powerful searchlights: he had found the *Westfalen*. In her wake followed *Nassau* and *Rheinland*. All three battleships opened fire, together with the light cruisers *Stuttgart* and *Hamburg* which found themselves sandwiched between the Dreadnoughts and the enemy destroyers.

Tipperary was blown to pieces by a hail of fire from *Westfalen*'s secondary armament. Her next astern, *Spitfire*, circled to starboard, intending to take off survivors. The British destroyers fired at the enemy searchlights and riddling the battleships' upperworks. *Westfalen*'s captain was wounded and *Rheinland* suffered 30 casualties, including ten dead from a single 4-in. (10 mm) shell. The three battleships turned hard to starboard, assuming the British had launched torpedoes, then swung back on their original course: this caught out *Spitfire* which found herself heading straight at *Nassau*. They met port bow to port bow in a grinding collision, heeling wildly. *Nassau* let fly with 'A' turret's 11-in. (280 mm) guns; the blast blew the destroyer's mast and forward funnel overboard and wrecked the bridge. Torn open along a third of her length, *Spitfire* nevertheless remained afloat.

The German light cruisers endeavoured to slip through the battleship line, but *Elbing* was rammed by *Posen* and ripped open below the waterline; her engine rooms flooded, she drifted helplessly as the High Sea Fleet forged onwards.

The rest of the 4th Destroyer Flotilla came up, led by Commander Allen in *Broke*. The grisly fate of *Tipperary* was repeated: he gave the

75

recognition signal to the strange battleships and was plastered with shells by *Westfalen*, *Rheinland* and the cruiser *Rostock*. Her next astern, *Sparrowhawk*, collided with her, and *Contest* sliced off *Sparrowhawk*'s stern. *Broke* and *Contest* limped off, but *Sparrowhawk* had to be abandoned the next day. Someone launched a torpedo: *Rostock* reeled from a hit in her No. 4 boiler room and was temporarily left without power. Reduced to a crawl and shipping nearly 1,000 tons of water, she followed in the wake of the fleet.

Just after midnight, the remaining five units of the 4th Destroyer Flotilla were seen from *Westfalen* which opened fire with her 5.9-in. (150 mm) guns. Her searchlights picked out the *Fortune*, which was sunk in less than a minute. *Rheinland*, *Posen*, *Oldenburg* and *Helgoland* all engaged; the destroyers firing back at the searchlights and launching torpedoes. The German squadron turned eight points together to starboard, combing the tracks. It was a near run for *Oldenburg*: her bridge was swept by shell splinters that mowed down 20 men. Despite injuries, Kapitän Hopfner stepped over the body of his helmsman to steer the ship clear.

The German battleships resumed their previous heading, *Nassau* steering to regain her position in the line. Suddenly a big ship emerged from the east and when challenged with the German recognition signal, she veered away. Four funnels: unmistakably one of the old British armoured cruisers. It was *Black Prince*, one of the survivors from Arbuthnot's ill-fated 1st Cruiser Squadron, presumably thinking she had found the British battle fleet and realising at the last moment she had made a terrible error. *Thüringen* illuminated her with searchlights and opened fire at little more than 1,000 yards (910 m). The shells burst inside her hull with horrific effect. Other battleships joined in, *Nassau*, *Ostfriesland* and even Scheer's flagship. 'It was so near,' the German admiral remembered, 'the crew could be seen rushing backwards and forwards on the burning deck while the searchlights disclosed the flight of the heavy projectiles till they fell and exploded.' *Black Prince* burned with a fierce light until after 10–15 minutes there was a massive explosion and she vanished, 'a grand but terrible sight'. There were no survivors. *Nassau* turned hard to starboard to avoid the wreck, narrowly avoiding collision with *Kaiserin*. At the same time, a lost destroyer from the dispersed 4th Flotilla blundered into the Germans. *Ardent* got off one torpedo but was caught in searchlights only 900 yards (819 m) away. *Westfalen* and *Posen* sank her in a few minutes.

While *Westfalen* hacked through the British flotillas, there were several skirmishes at the rear of the German line. At 0012hrs three German destroyers were ordered to investigate a burning ship that turned out to be the wrecked *Tipperary*. *S 53* rescued nine survivors from a nearby raft then located the crippled *Elbing* and stood by her, after a quick exchange of shots and torpedoes with a British straggler, *Broke*. *G 88* also fired on *Broke* but the Germans left their opponent, which only had one gun left in action. *Tipperary* did not sink until some time later, the survivors still aboard were rescued by *Sparrowhawk*. *S 52* was looking for the *Lützow* but found the 11th Destroyer Flotilla at very close range – *Castor* tried to ram her – but she escaped, making smoke.

At about 0035hrs *Westfalen* spotted more British destroyers 1,100 yards (1,000 m) off her port bow and a suspicious cloud of smoke

The *Seydlitz* was barely afloat by the early hours of 1 June, only extensive counter-flooding kept her from capsizing. With barely a gun still in action, she limped home alone, observed by several unenterprising British captains. Her survival was testimony to the strength of her construction and an exceptionally well-trained crew. (IWM)

to starboard. Officers on *Rheinland* thought British light discipline was poor and the black colour of the British ships made them stand out at night. (They were repainted grey, like their opponents, after the battle.) It was the 9th and 13th Flotillas plus *Unity* from the 4th. *Westfalen* turned to ram, forcing *Petard* to take evasive action and curse the fact she had expended her torpedoes earlier. The battleship's secondary armament raked her and caused a spectacular fuel-oil fire, leading the Germans to claim her as sunk. In fact, she escaped. *Turbulent*, following *Petard*, was not so fortunate: *Westfalen*'s port secondary batteries shot her to pieces and she was left sinking. *V 71* and *V 73* closed to rescue survivors, *V 71* administering the coup de grâce with a torpedo. British destroyers *Narborough* and *Pelican* both had torpedoes, but did not attack, mistaking the German battleships for British cruisers.

In the early hours of 1 June, the wind freshened from the south-south-west, hastening the end of the *Lützow*. The battle cruiser was so far down forward that her propellers came out of the water. Her electrical power failed by midnight, leaving her crew to work by oil lamps and candles. Just before 0100hrs the escorting destroyers *G 40*, *G 38*, *V 45* and *G 37* were called to come alongside and take off her crew. *G 38* sank her with a torpedo at 0145hrs. Elsewhere in the darkness, *Elbing* drifted, unable to restart her turbines. Kapitän Madlung and a skeleton crew remained aboard after *S 53* took off the rest of her people. They rigged a sail, intending to make for Denmark, but British destroyers were seen at 0200hrs and Madlung ordered his team into the cutter and scuttled his ship. They picked up a survivor from *Tipperary* before they in turn were rescued by a Dutch trawler after dawn.

Wiesbaden foundered sometime before first light. How many of her gallant crew made it into the water remains unknown. Only one man survived to be found by a passing Norwegian ship on the afternoon of 2 June. Jellicoe expressed his admiration for the conduct of her people, noting that even under fire from a whole battle fleet, her solitary working gun remained in action.

No news of these night-time clashes reached Admiral Jellicoe. Very few of his captains even thought to inform him what they had seen. Symptomatic was the story aboard *Malaya*, rearmost battleship of the 5th Battle Squadron, which enjoyed a grandstand view of *Westfalen* in action with the 4th Destroyer Flotilla. Her big guns were trained on *Westfalen* but the captain forbade the gunnery officer's pleas to open fire

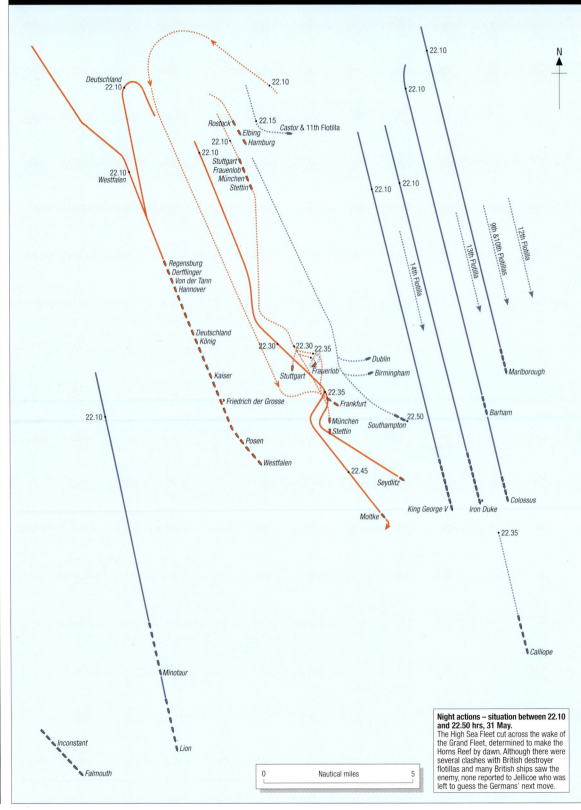

N

Deutschland
22.10

Westfalen
22.10

22.10

Rostock
Elbing
Hamburg
22.10
22.10
Stuttgart
Frauenlob
München
Stettin

22.15

Castor & 11th Flotilla

22.10

22.10

22.10

22.10

12th Flotilla

9th & 10th Flotillas

13th Flotilla

14th Flotilla

Regensburg
Derfflinger
Von der Tann
Hannover

Deutschland
König

Kaiser

Friedrich der Grosse

22.30   22.30 22.35
Stuttgart   Frauerlob

Dublin

Birmingham

Marlborough

22.10

Posen

Westfalen

22.35
Frankfurt

München
Stettin   Southampton

22.50

Barham

22.45

Seydlitz

King George V   Iron Duke   Colossus

Moltke

22.35

Minotaur

Calliope

Inconstant

Lion

Falmouth

0   Nautical miles   5

**Night actions – situation between 22.10
and 22.50 hrs, 31 May.**
The High Sea Fleet cut across the wake of
the Grand Fleet, determined to make the
Horns Reef by dawn. Although there were
several clashes with British destroyer
flotillas and many British ships saw the
enemy, none reported to Jellicoe who was
left to guess the Germans' next move.

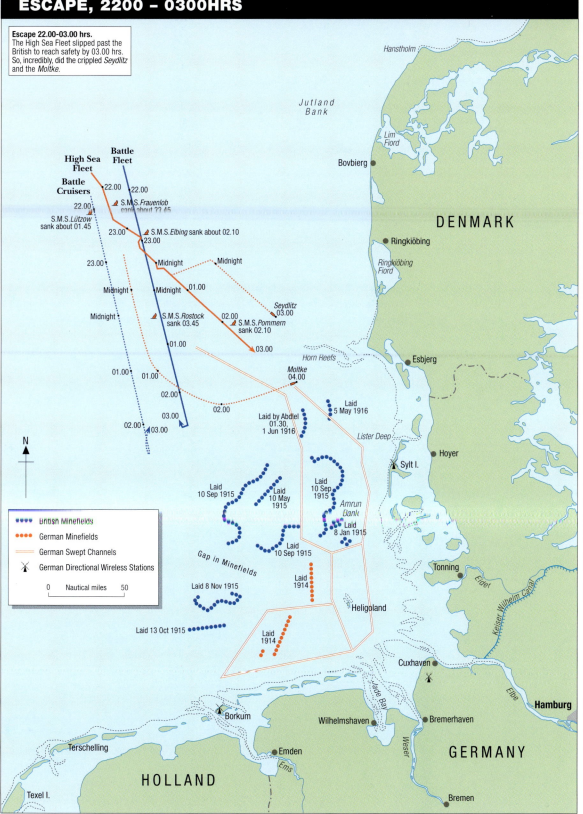

ESCAPE, 2200 – 0300HRS

Escape 22.00-03.00 hrs.
The High Sea Fleet slipped past the British to reach safety by 03.00 hrs. So, incredibly, did the crippled *Seydlitz* and the *Moltke*.

Hanstholm

Jutland Bank

Lim Fiord

Bovbierg

DENMARK

High Sea Fleet 22.00 | 22.00 **Battle Fleet**

Battle Cruisers 22.00

S.M.S.*Frauenlob* sank about 23.45

S.M.S.*Lützow* sank about 01.45

Ringkiöbing

23.00 | S.M.S.*Elbing* sank about 02.10
23.00

23.00

Midnight | Midnight

Ringkiöbing Fiord

Midnight | Midnight | 01.00

Midnight | *Seydlitz* 03.00

Midnight | S.M.S.*Rostock* sank 03.45 | 02.00
S.M.S.*Pommern* sank 02.10

01.00 | 03.00

Horn Reefs | Esbjerg

Moltke 04.00

01.00 | 01.00 | 02.00

02.00 | 03.00

02.00 | 03.00

Laid 5 May 1916

Laid by Abdiel 01.30, 1 Jun 1916

Lister Deep

Sylt I.

Hoyer

Laid 10 Sep 1915

Laid 10 May 1915

Laid 10 Sep 1915

Amrun Bank

Laid 8 Jan 1915

Laid 10 Sep 1915

N

Gap in Minefields

Laid 1914

Tonning

Laid 8 Nov 1915

Laid 1914

Heligoland

•••• British Minefields

•••• German Minefields

━━ German Swept Channels

⚡ German Directional Wireless Stations

0   Nautical miles   50

Laid 13 Oct 1915

Laid 1914

Elder

Keiser Wilhelm Canal

Cuxhaven

Elbe

Hamburg

Borkum

Wilhelmshaven

Bremerhaven

GERMANY

Terschelling

Jade Bay

Weser

HOLLAND

Emden

Ems

Bremen

Texel I.

81

The Nassau class Dreadnought *Posen* wore the flag of Konteradmiral Engelhardt at Jutland. She collided with the German cruiser *Elbing* when the light forces attempted to slip through the battle line during the night actions. *Elbing* was unable to restore power and was eventually scuttled. *Posen* and *Westfalen* sank the British destroyer *Ardent* which attempted to torpedo them. (IWM)

on the grounds that Rear-Admiral Evan-Thomas was only two ships ahead and if he wanted *Malaya* to shoot he would surely signal her to do so. Captain Waller of the *Barham* saw everything too, but later justified his – and his admiral's – dull passivity on the grounds that the commander-in-chief would not want to be burdened with a stream of 'superfluous' signals. He did not want to use the radio in case the Germans detected the transmission and located the fleet!

That spirited fighting sailor of the Second World War, Captain Donald Macintyre, notes in his study of Jutland that even Captain Thompson of the *Petard* (who had not only found the German battleships but come perilously close to being sunk in the process) failed to pass on what he had seen. 'If the intelligence and understanding of the flag and commanding officers had matched their gallantry and devotion, the story of Jutland might have been very different.' The British sailed blithely on. On *Iron Duke* the flashes and bangs astern were assumed to be the anticipated German torpedo attack meeting the British destroyers. Had anyone told Jellicoe German battleships were there, he would have known at once they were heading for the Horns Reef.

The Admiralty knew. Room 40 had intercepted a succession of radio signals that betrayed Scheer's intentions: his request for airship reconnaissance at first light over the Horns Reef and Kommodore Michelson's signal for the German torpedo boat flotillas to rendezvous with the battle fleet at the Horns Reef at 0300hrs. Four position reports transmitted from Scheer's flagship would have enabled his course to be plotted exactly. But the Admiralty passed on only one German signal, giving the course, speed and position of the High Sea Fleet. Jellicoe had lost faith in their reports after the previous errors – position reports that conflicted with signals from his own captains engaging the enemy. Had the Admiralty passed on all the intercepts instead of sitting on the ones that positively identified Scheer's escape route, Jellicoe would have intercepted the German fleet at daylight off the Horns Reef on 1 June.

The last major clash occurred at about 0200hrs when the British 12th Destroyer Flotilla observed a line of battleships to starboard, soon identified as Kaiser class. The destroyers closed the enemy at 25 knots in the half-light of pre-dawn. The section of the German line they had

Black Prince survived the destruction of the rest of her squadron during the afternoon but her movements thereafter are largely conjecture. Shortly after midnight she approached the German battle line and was illuminated by the *Thüringen's* searchlights before she could escape. At a range of no more than 1,000 yards (910 m), she was engaged by up to five Dreadnoughts including Scheer's flagship. The German admiral described how 'the crew could be seen rushing backwards and forwards on the burning deck while the searchlights disclosed the flight of the heavy projectiles till they fell and exploded'. Ablaze from end to end, *Black Prince* blew up with the loss of all hands. (IWM)

encountered consisted of the four König-class Dreadnoughts followed by II Geschwader with the errant *Nassau* tucked in the middle of the six pre-Dreadnoughts. The battleships expected to see German torpedo boats and were exchanging recognition signals with their own flotillas to starboard when they saw other destroyers to port. *Markgraf* thought they were German and held her fire, but *König's* secondary armament roared into action and *Grosser Kurfürst* followed suit. The König class turned away as the British launched a total of 12 torpedoes, eight at the Dreadnoughts and four, all from the *Obedient*, at II Geschwader. One passed close ahead of *Grosser Kurfürst*, another exploded in the wake of the *Kronprinz* while observers on *Markgraf* saw a track race past on a parallel course within 100 feet (30 m). *Obedient* was more successful: one or two of her torpedoes struck *Pommern*, two columns of flame shooting as high as her mastheads. Several sharp detonations were followed by a massive explosion that broke her in two. *Hannover* passed the spot a few minutes later and all that remained was her stern section, floating upside down. None of the 844 officers and men aboard survived. A further five torpedoes were fired as the rest of the 12th Flotilla came up, but they scored no hits as the Germans turned away, secondary armaments blazing.

Fifteen minutes later, the Germans thought they were under attack again. The destroyer *V 4* had her bows blown off. There are no plausible torpedo firings that tie in with her position – she was with *V 2* and *V 6* off the starboard beam of I Geschwader. Presumably it was a drifting mine. Eighteen men were killed and four injured; the rest of her crew were taken off and the *V 4* finished off with a torpedo.

Disappointment at dawn

The first German the British battle cruisers saw was the Zeppelin *L 11* which emerged from the cloud base at about 0330hrs. The airship received a hot reception, some of the battle cruisers firing their main armament at her. Jellicoe received the crushing news that the Germans had escaped when *Iron Duke* took in a signal from the Admiralty giving the High Sea Fleet's position, course and speed at 0230hrs – Scheer had escaped via the Horns Reef.

OVERLEAF **Ramming attack. The moment of impact, when the port bows of the destroyer *Spitfire* and *Nassau* collided. *Nassau* blasted *Spitfire* with her guns on 'A' turret, blowing apart *Spitfire's* mast and forward funnel, and knocking out the bridge. *Spitfire* somehow remained afloat, despite being torn open along a third of her length, with 20ft of *Nassau's* side plating attached to her bows.**

The Grand Fleet swept the battle area, hoping at least to find the *Lützow*, but nothing remained apart from bodies and floating wreckage. Visibility at dawn was about 5,000 yards (4,550 m), and no better from the air than at sea level. Scheer was alarmed to receive a signal from the airship *L 24*, locating the British fleet close to the Danish coast off Hanstholm, but what she actually saw remains a mystery. *L 11* did find the British and shadowed them for nearly an hour until the anti-aircraft fire became too close for comfort and she made off north-east with the wind behind her. The size of a battleship, her bulk attracted everything from 3-pdrs. to 15-in. (381 mm) guns at full elevation.

The last stages of the German retreat were marked by the same ' submarine' sightings. At least six battleships fired on these imaginary submarines; *Hannover* reported seeing a submarine in the act of submerging. It seemed that their fears were confirmed at 0520hrs when *Ostfriesland* was stricken by an explosion on her starboard side, but her crew found bits of mine on her quarterdeck. The *Abdiel*'s mines had claimed their first, but only, victim. *Kaiser* dropped a mine buoy to mark the danger area and Scheer ordered the fleet to hold its course. Two of the pre-Dreadnoughts mistook the buoy for a periscope and fired several rounds of 11 in (280 mm) main armament at it.

There were three British submarines lying in wait: *E 55*, *E 26* and *D 1*. Acting under their original orders for 2 June, they did not maintain a continuous watch on 1 June. The *E 6* was off the Vyl lightship by 0100hrs on 1 June and was close to where the High Sea Fleet passed three hours later, but never saw anything. *E 55* was off the Horns Reef about midnight when a lookout shouted that there was a Zeppelin overhead. The submarine's commander recalled, 'I looked up and saw a man put his head out the car of a Zepp, so I blew the hooter and dived to the bottom.' *E 55* remained there, listening to distant depth-charging, surfacing in the morning to find nothing. The submarine returned without incident to Harwich, ignorant of the battle. When asked by an excited torpedo lieutenant at the depot ship 'how many ships did you get', they thought he was joking. *D 1* saw nothing until the evening of 2 June, when she fired a single torpedo at the German submarine *U 64* which she spotted on the surface. It missed.

Ironically, in view of Jellicoe's assumption the Germans would lay mines in their wake, the only minelayer at Jutland was HMS *Abdiel*. Jellicoe despatched her during the night to mine the Germans' route home and at 0520 hrs the *Ostfriesland* struck one. (Author's Collection)

With over 1,000 survivors from *Lützow* crammed aboard, *G 40, G 38, V 45* and *G 37* were unfortunate to run into four British destroyers at 0330hrs However, they were on opposite courses and the visibility remained poor. The Germans fired three torpedoes, none of which found their mark, nor did their gunnery achieve much although the British did little better. *G 40* suffered a hit from a 6-in. shell that damaged one of her turbines and she lost speed after a few minutes, being taken in tow by *G 37*.

The cruiser *Dublin* caught the *S 54, V 71* and *V 73* taking the crew off the *Rostock* just before 0400hrs but the *S 54* made the first part of the British night recognition signal ('UA') which had been observed by several German ships that night. The Germans were hurrying because they had heard *L 11*'s signal that placed the British battle fleet dangerously close to them. *S 54* led *Dublin* away and gave her the slip. The two other German destroyers completed the rescue of *Rostock*'s crew and torpedoed the wreck.

Warrior was towed by the *Engadine* for nearly 100 miles (161 km) until the swell increased and the big cruiser no longer answered the motion of the sea. Water washed over her upper deck. At 0715hrs it was decided to take off her crew, a delicate business given the state of the cruiser and the size of the *Engadine*. It was managed with commendable discipline. Flight Lieutenant Rutland dived in to rescue a wounded man who slipped from his stretcher and fell between the ships. It was a brave act that won him the Albert Medal although, sadly, the wounded sailor died.

The Grand Fleet turned for home, also shadowed by phantom submarines. However, several detached vessels met real submarines. In the forenoon *Marlborough* saw two U-boats', conning towers awash some 8 miles (13 km) off — actually the British *G 3* and *G 5*, but she did not stay to find out. *Minotaur* claimed to have sunk a U-boat on the evening of 2 June, but her target was the British *E 30* out of Blyth and she survived. At 0935hrs on 1 June *U 51* fired a torpedo at what her skipper thought was a Canopus class pre-Dreadnought: it was the *Warspite*, returning alone to Rosyth. He missed from 650 yards, the battleship lucky the *U 51*'s other bow tube malfunctioned. Met by torpedo boats from Rosyth just before 1200hrs, *Warspite* sighted the periscope of another U-boat. Her captain rang down for emergency speed and turned to ram, sending *U 63* crash-diving for safety. The submarine bottomed at 160 feet (48.5m), porpoised to the surface and attracted four rounds from the battleship's 6-in. (150 mm) guns before vanishing again. She subsequently got away, despite depth-charging by submarine chasers.

AFTERMATH

Jellicoe did not learn of the sinking of *Queen Mary* and *Indefatigable* until Beatty sent him a signal timed at 1000 hrs – terrible news that compounded his sense of failure. It was plain that the Royal Navy had suffered heavy casualties and far from clear that the Germans had lost any major units. Nevertheless, Jellicoe had an operational fleet in the North Sea the morning after Jutland. Scheer did not.

The German battle cruiser squadron was reduced to *Moltke*. Three of the four Königs were unable to make full speed. Had Jellicoe been off the Horns Reef at dawn, it is difficult to see how Scheer could have escaped, even in the morning rain that reduced visibility to a couple of miles.

Seydlitz was towed into port backwards, counter-flooding increasing the quantity of water inside her to over 5,000 tons. She was dangerously unstable on 2 June when the wind got up to Force 8. The wounded were taken off, and she crossed the bar of the Jade Basin on that morning's high tide. Docked on 6 June, she was under repair until 16 September. All the other damaged German capital ships were repaired by the first week of August, except for *Derfflinger* which did not leave Kiel dockyard until 15 October.

Most of the damaged British ships were ready for action by the end of June, although *Princess Royal* was repaired at Portsmouth from 13 June to 15 July. *Lion* was restored to operational readiness without 'Q' turret, which was refitted at Armstrong's on the Tyne from 6–23 September.

The balance sheet showed British losses as 6,094 dead, 674 wounded and 177 prisoners-of-war; German casualties were 2,551 dead, 507 wounded and no prisoners. The following ships had been sunk:

British
Battle cruisers: *Queen Mary, Indefatigable, Invincible*
Armoured cruisers: *Defence, Warrior, Black Prince*
Destroyers: *Tipperary, Nestor, Nomad, Turbulent, Ardent, Fortune, Shark, Sparrowhawk*

German
Battle cruiser: *Lützow*
Pre-Dreadnought: *Pommern*
Light cruisers: *Wiesbaden, Elbing Rostock, Frauenlob*
Destroyers: *V 48, S 35, V 29, V 27, V 4*

The truth is down there
Perhaps the reason the British found the news of Jutland hard to swallow was that the Germans were in port claiming victory while the Admiralty remained ominously quiet. The kaiser wallowed in reflected glory. 'Now', he announced, 'the magic of Trafalgar has been broken'. He toured the fleet on 5 June, showering Iron Crosses in his wake. Scheer

was promoted admiral, although he refused to be ennobled, and was never the 'Von Scheer' of some British accounts. Hipper was not so reticent, and accepted his sovereign's offer to become Ritter von Hipper.[20]

The balance sheet was strongly in Germany's favour, and this was milked mercilessly, although the effect was reduced when news of *Lützow*'s loss leaked out. However, Scheer's bombastic victory pronouncements were for public consumption. To his kaiser he was brutally candid. Germany, he said, could never win a surface engagement with the British. The only hope of victory at sea was an unrestricted U-boat campaign. Von Tirpitz's 'risk theory' was a busted flush.

Germany resumed unrestricted submarine warfare in February 1917 and brought the United States into the war against her. That summer there were serious disturbances throughout the High Sea Fleet: boredom, bad food and draconian discipline provoked open mutiny. It did not help that many of the best junior officers left the capital ships to serve in submarines, leaving the martinets to lord it from the

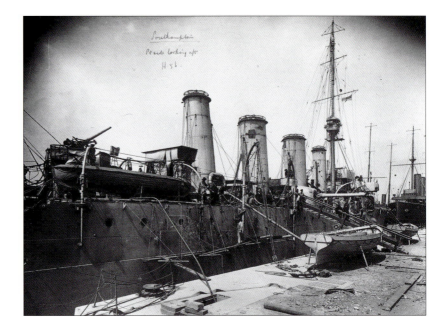

Southampton docked after the battle. Note the splinter damage to her funnels. Reaction to the battle varied from port to port, with some sailors getting pelted with coal by dockside labourers 'for losing'. Clumsy public relations by the Admiralty seemed to support German claims of a victory in the North Sea. (IWM)

quarterdeck. The fleet mutinied in April 1918 rather than embark on a 'suicide sortie' intended to salvage the honour of the officer class.

Jellicoe's report to the Admiralty remains the best one-sentence summary of Jutland and should be remembered when examining maps of the battle: 'The whole situation was difficult to grasp, as I had no real idea of what was going on and we could hardly see anything except flashes of guns, shells falling, ships blowing up and an occasional glimpse of an enemy vessel.' It was galling that the enemy had escaped, but Jellicoe was not disposed to take risks merely to confirm the existing strategic situation, namely that the Germans were locked into the North Sea. Of the Germans, Jellicoe remarked with his characteristic courtesy, 'The enemy fought with the gallantry that was expected of him, and showed humanity in rescuing officers and men from the water.'

One of the Queen Elizabeth class under repair. *Barham* and *Malaya* were back with the fleet by 8 and 11 July respectively, although *Warspite* was in dockyard hands until 20 July. (IWM)

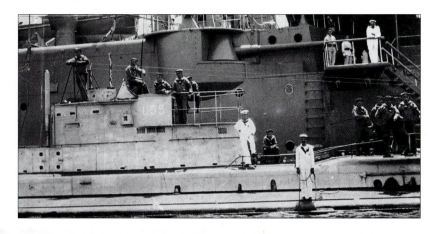

Scheer enjoyed a great reputation after Jutland, largely, but not entirely, based on his own account of events.[21] Posterity has not been so kind. Arthur Marder's judgement stands: 'He had a very bad off-day at Jutland, since every time he came within sight of the British fleet, he did so by accident and was so completely taken by surprise that on each occasion he found the British battle line across his "T".' Could he have done better? Had events gone in his favour, he might have savaged a detached British squadron, but it is difficult to imagine the Grand Fleet being massacred in some sort of North Sea Tsushima. The British battle fleet had a sufficient margin of superiority to survive even a bad defeat.

Beatty succeeded Jellicoe as Commander-in-Chief of the Grand Fleet when the latter was promoted to First Sea Lord in 1917. The reputations of both men are hard to disentangle thanks to partisan accounts from their own officers and the efforts of the 'Beatty school' to massage the *Official History* in favour of their man. It was an ugly business and the details need not detain us here. It was fatal for Beatty's flag lieutenant Ralph Seymour: he tried to marry Beatty's step-niece but was ordered to direct his attentions elsewhere. Seymour committed suicide in 1922 by throwing himself off Beachy Head.

The usual criticism of Jellicoe is that he should have been more aggressive. Had he taken greater risks, he could have routed the High Sea Fleet. The strategic result would have been the same, however. Jellicoe's caution and the tactical inflexibility of the Royal Navy have been the theme of many a Jutland book, but the idea he was a worrier, not a warrior, is an exaggeration. It is worth considering an alternative: that 'Balaklava Beatty' (as Fisher christened him after Jutland) might have come a cropper during his intervention off Heligoland in 1914 – a disaster that would probably have been explained in terms of outdated offensive attitudes, traceable to the public school system and the fox-hunting mentality of the upper classes.

Reinhard Scheer died in 1928, just after he had accepted Jellicoe's invitation to come and stay with him in England. What an intriguing dinner conversation that would have been. Hipper succeeded Scheer in command of the High Sea Fleet in 1917 and had the distasteful experience of watching his once proud fleet steam to surrender with mutinous sailors in charge. Jellicoe died in November 1935, Beatty in March 1936. Do they foregather, Donald Macintyre speculated, 'in some naval Valhalla, to argue out the old question, "Who won at Jutland?"'

CHRONOLOGY

30 May 1916

1716hrs Grand Fleet ordered to put to sea that night to intercept German sortie detected by signals intelligence.

2230hrs Grand Fleet puts to sea.

0030hrs Admiral Jackson asks Room 40 where German callsign 'DK' is placed. The answer, 'in the Jade' sets in train the Admiralty's disastrous failure to pass on priceless signals intelligence.

31 May 1916

0100hrs German battle cruisers put to sea.

0200hrs High Sea Fleet puts to sea.

1400hrs *Elbing* sights the Danish steamer *N.J. Fjord* and sends torpedo boats *B 109* and *B 110* to investigate. The same steamer attracts the attention of *Galatea* and *Phaeton*.

1428hrs *Galatea* and *Phaeton* open fire on the German torpedo boats.

1451hrs British and German battle cruisers sight each other.

1548hrs *Lützow* opens fire at 16,840 yards (15,400 m). The British battle cruisers return fire.

1503hrs *Indefatigable* explodes and sinks.

1611hrs 5th Battle Squadron opens fire.

1620hrs Flotillas clash: *Nomad* and *V 29* and *V 27* sunk.

1646hrs High Sea Fleet in sight of the rival battle cruisers. British turn away, beginning the 'run to the north'.

1648hrs *Wiesbaden* hit and left unable to manoeuvre.

1700hrs Jellicoe signals the Admiralty: 'Fleet action is imminent'.

1815hrs *Shark* sunk. Jellicoe orders Grand Fleet to deploy.

1825hrs *Defence* blows up as the armoured cruisers charge the German battle line. Grand Fleet deploys and engages sections of the German line.

1833hrs *Invincible* engages *Derfflinger* and is blown up.

1835hrs High Sea Fleet performs its *Gefechtskehrwendung* (about turn) manoeuvre and escapes into the murk.

1847hrs *Lützow* signals that she cannot keep her place in the line, damage from *Invincible*'s last broadside proves fatal. Hipper is taken off by *G 39*.

1855hrs Scheer turns the High Sea Fleet again and heads back, unknowingly into the Grand Fleet.

1905hrs High Sea Fleet in sight of Grand Fleet again: British ships all but invisible to the Germans who suffer repeated hits.

1913hrs Scheer orders 'death ride' of the battle cruisers.

1915hrs Scheer orders massed attack by torpedo boats.

1916hrs Third 'about turn' by High Sea Fleet.

2030hrs Final shots between British battle cruisers and German battle cruisers and pre-Dreadnoughts.

2235hrs *Frauenlob* sunk.

2335hrs *Tipperary* sunk by German Dreadnoughts.

1 June

2350–0005hrs *Ardent* and *Fortune* sunk by German battleships, *Sparrowhawk* badly damaged.

0020hrs Armoured cruiser *Black Prince* blunders into German battle line and is sunk with all hands.

0105hrs *Westfalen* sinks the destroyer *Turbulent*.

0147hrs On the brink of foundering, *Lützow* is scuttled and her crew taken off.

0200–0215hrs *Elbing* scuttled, crew taken off. Pre-Dreadnought *Pommern* torpedoed and sunk with all hands. *V 4* blown up by mine or torpedo.

0520hrs *Ostfriesland* mined.

1500hrs *Friedrich der Große* anchors in Wilhelmshaven.

SELECT BIBLIOGRAPHY

OPPOSITE, LEFT **Kaiser** steams to surrender at Scapa Flow in November 1918. The High Sea Fleet mutinied when Admiral Hipper attempted to order a suicide sortie against the Grand Fleet. Although some officers were retained, control of the ships was now in the hands of sailors' soviets (committees). (IWM)

OPPOSITE, RIGHT **Derfflinger** sinks at Scapa Flow after the Germans scuttled the surrendered ships rather than hand them over. The British Admiralty was quietly relieved at not having to deal with demands from the French, Italian and other Allied navies for a share in the captured fleet. (IWM)

Max Arthur, *The Royal Navy, A Narrative History,* 1914–39, Hodder & Stoughton, 1996

Patrick Beesly, *Room 40: British Naval Intelligence 1914–18*, Hamish Hamilton, 1982

Geoffrey Bennett, *The Battle of Jutland*, David & Charles, 1964

Geoffrey Bennett, *The Naval Battles of the First World War*, Pan, 1974

Nicholas Campbell, *Jutland: An Analysis of the Fighting*, Conway, 1986

W. S. Chalmers, *Life and Letters of David Earl Beatty*, Hodder & Stoughton, 1951

Winston Churchill, *World Crisis*, London, 1923

Conway's *All the World's Fighting Ships* 1906–21, London 1985

Julian Corbett, *Naval Operations*, Vols.1–III, London 1920

Harold Fawcett & Geoffrey Cooper, *The Fighting at Jutland*, Macmillan, 1921

Lord Fisher of Kilverstone, *Memories*, London 1919

Bernard Fitzsimmons (Ed), *Warships & Sea Battles of World War I*, Phoebus/BPC Publishing, 1973

Langhorne Gibson & John Harper, *The Riddle of Jutland*, Cassell, 1934

James Goldrick, *The King's Ships were at Sea,* Navy Institute Press, 1984

Erich Gröner, *Die deutschen Kriegsschiffe 1815–1945*, Bernard & Graefe Verlag, 1982

Otto Groos, *Der Krieg in der Nordsee*, Mittler, 1920

John Harper, *The Truth about Jutland*, Murray, 1927

Georg von Hase, *Kiel and Jutland*, Skeffington, 1921

Holger Herwig, *Luxury Fleet*, Allen & Unwin, 1980

Hans Hildebrand, *Albert Röhr & Hans-Otto Steinmetz, Die Deutschen Kriegsschiffe—ein Spiegel der Marinegeschichte von 1815 bis zur Gegegenwart* (7 volumes), Koehlers Verlagsgesellschaft, 1980–85

Richard Hough, *The Great War at Sea*, Oxford University Press, 1983

Bernard Ireland & Tony Gibbons, *Jane's Battleships of the 20th Century*, HarperCollins, 1996

Viscount Jellicoe, *The Grand Fleet 1914–16*, Cassell, 1919

Viscount Jellicoe, *C-in-C's Narrative of the Action with the German Fleet off Jutland, 1916*

Narrative of the Battle of Jutland, HMSO, 1924

Battle of Jutland: Official Despatches, HMSO, 1920

Donald Macintyre, *Jutland*, Pan, 1960

Arthur Marder, *From Dreadnought to Scapa Flow*, Oxford University Press, 5 Volumes, 1961-70

Robert Massie, *Dreadnought*, Jonathan Cape, 1992

Peter Padfield, *Aim Straight: A biography of Admiral Sir Percy Scott*, Hodder & Stoughton, 1966

Oscar Parkes, *British Battleships*, London, 1970

Anthony Pollen, *The Great Gunnery Scandal*, Collins, 1980

Stephen Roskill, *Churchill and the Admirals*, Collins, 1977

Stephen Roskill, *Earl Beatty*, Collins, 1981

Jon Sumida, *In Defense of Naval Supremacy*, London, 1989

'Taffrail' (Henry Dorling), *Endless Story*, Hodder & Stoughton, 1931

V. E. Tarrant, *Jutland, The German Perspective*, Arms & Armour, 1995

V. E. Tarrant, *Invincible, The Story of the First Battle Cruiser*, Arms & Armour, 1986

INDEX

FOOTNOTES

1   Holger Herwig, *Luxury Fleet* (London 1980), p56.
2   *Naval Review*, 5, 191.7
3   Ibid.
4   *The Fighting at Jutland*, London 1921, p35.
5   For a thorough discussion of this incident, see Andrew Gordon, *The Rules of the Game*, Murray 1996,
        pp 81–101.
6   Winston Churchill, *The Great War* Vol II, p 847.
7   Official report of the reconnaissance flight, reprinted in *The Fighting at Jutland*, London 1921.
8   Georg von Hase, *Kiel and Jutland*, London, 1921, p81.
9   Von Hase, p83.
10 See John Campbell, *Jutland: an analysis of the fighting*, p66. He says Captain Chatfield ordered the magazine flooded after the hit and the transmitting station queried the order because 'A' magazine had been flooded in error during the battle of Dogger Bank. The later fire and explosion killed members of the damage control party too. However, *Lion*'s gunnery officer, quoted in *The Fighting at Jutland*. p 65. says the order was given by Major Harvey, that it was promptly carried out and credits him with saving the ship.
11 W.S. Chalmers, *The Life and letters of David Lord Beatty*, London, 1951.
12 *The Fighting at Jutland,* p 43.
13 Responsibility for this error, which could have led to the loss of one or more of the Queen Elizabeths, has been bitterly contested since the 1920s. See Andrew Gordon's analysis in *Rules of the Game*, pp 129–151.
14 *The Grand Fleet 1914–16* Admiral Viscount Jellicoe of Scapa, London 1919, p 345.
15 Max Arthur, *The Royal Navy* 1914–39, Hodder & Stoughton, 1996.
16 Reinhard Scheer, *Germany's High Sea Fleet in the World War*, 1920
17 Von Hase, Op. Cit.
18 *The Fighting at Jutland,* p 86.
19 Vice-Admiral B.B. Schofield (a midshipman on *Indomitable*) quoted in James Goldrick, *The King's Ships were at Sea* (Annapolis, 1984).
20 He was knighted by the king of Bavaria on 6 June.
21 Richard Hough described Scheer's memoirs as 'egocentric, idiosyncratic, unreliable and execrably translated, but should be read'.

3/υ